HIS WEIRD AND WANTON WAYS

The Secret Life of Howard Hughes

BY THE SAME AUTHOR

THREE CARS IN EVERY GARAGE

FAITH, CULTS AND SECTS OF AMERICA

THE ETERNAL SEARCH

HIS WEIRD AND WANTON WAYS

The Secret Life of Howard Hughes

by RICHARD MATHISON

WILLIAM MORROW AND COMPANY, INC. | NEW YORK 1977

Printed in the United States of America.

1 2 3 4 5 6 7 8 9 10

Library of Congress Cataloging in Publication Data

Mathison, Richard R
His weird and wanton ways, the secret life of Howard Hughes.

1. Hughes, Howard Robard, 1905-1976. 2. Millionaires—Biography.
CT275.H6678M38 670'.9'24 [B] 76-51728
ISBN 0-688-03170-6

BOOK DESIGN CARL WEISS

To the loyal and patient people

who worked for Howard Hughes

during the years he was busy

with an interesting variety

of vital matters

HIS WEIRD AND WANTON WAYS

The Secret Life of Howard Hughes

CHAPTER 1

In the fall of 1949 Howard Hughes decided he needed a home in Las Vegas. His scouts found a huge, rambling ranch house and he leased it. But he feared the sand and dust. He ordered a crew of engineers at Hughes Aircraft Company to design an air-conditioning plant. They built an addition to the house, containing the largest dehumidifier and dust filter in all Nevada. It took months and cost more than $80,000. Finally it was ready. Hughes arrived with his cook, Bruno. They settled in that morning. Bruno went to the kitchen to prepare Hughes' routine luncheon: a salad, small steak, and tomato juice washed down with Poland Spring water imported from Maine.

Hughes sat down at the dining room table and Bruno brought in the steak and salad.

Hughes glared at the salad. "Bruno, this goddamned thing is wilted," he complained. "Didn't you bring fresh lettuce?"

Bruno stared at his salad. "It was fresh," he stammered.

"It can't be, dammit!"

Bruno tried again with the same results. The dehumidifier was so powerful that the house was nearly at zero humidity.

By the time Bruno got the salad from the kitchen to the dining room it was too late.

Hughes got up in a rage. "To hell with this goddamned Vegas. It's too dusty anyway. Let's go!"

Bruno agreed. Hughes and Bruno locked the door and drove away. The Hughes organization continued to lease the house as there was a standing order that no one was ever to ask Hughes about a house until he told his executives to get rid of it.

Seven years later someone went to check out the house. The plates were still on the table with green mold in them. The forty-five minutes Howard Hughes spent in that house had cost more than a quarter million dollars.

That same memorable day he'd gone to the Flamingo and checked into a suite. Shortly after, he'd called his security man, Jeff Chouinard, in Los Angeles, and ordered him to report to Las Vegas. "I want you to be ready to go to Miami," he explained curtly. Chouinard arrived, checked in at the Desert Inn, and called Hughes, who told him to stand by.

Four days later Hughes called the detective back. "When are you leaving?" he asked.

"I haven't made a reservation yet," Chouinard replied, as usual wondering what the Old Man was into this time, why he had asked such a question without an explanation of why Chouinard was being asked to go.

"Make one and call me back," Hughes said.

Chouinard called the Old Man after he'd arranged for a noon flight. Hughes grunted and hung up, still without explaining the reason for the trip to Miami.

Ten minutes later the phone rang. "I just changed that flight to four o'clock," Hughes announced. There was then a long pause the detective suspected meant that another devious Hughes choreography of some sort was afoot.

"What time is checkout time?"

"I don't know," Chouinard replied.

"You ought to always find out about things like that. Find out and call me back."

Chouinard checked the desk and called Hughes back. "One o'clock," he reported.

"Good!" Hughes replied triumphantly. "Stay there until twelve forty-six but have your bags packed and be ready. Check out exactly at one o'clock. I've called a limousine and it will be in front. Come over here to the Flamingo. The bell captain is expecting you and will take care of your things. Stay in the lobby until about three forty-five, when it's time to go to the airport. But check with me before you do. The limousine will wait in front."

At 3:40 Chouinard called Hughes from the lobby, told him he was ready to leave, and asked him what he was to do in Miami.

"Don't worry about that. . . . You're five minutes early by the way. . . . I'll call you when you get there. Did you get checked out of the Desert Inn all right?"

Chouinard said he had.

A conspiratorial tone came into Hughes' voice. "Did they try to charge you for an extra day?"

"No, sir."

"How much were you paying?"

"Six dollars a day," Chouinard said.

"Good! We tricked the sons of bitches! If you'd stayed one more minute those bastards would probably have tried to collect for another day!"

CHAPTER 2

How Chouinard ever became a private detective and head of security for Hughes is as confusing and bewildering as his nearly two decades of working for him. Chouinard saw Howard Hughes through a distorted mirror and his own limited perspective. He knew little of the business activities and intrigues in which Hughes was involved—huge investments of endless millions of dollars. It was as if some Greek diety—a dour, lanky one in unpressed pants with dark eyes and an endless capacity for nagging—had twisted the world twenty degrees off tilt and told all his aides to live on it.

Chouinard believes that he was closer to Hughes personally over those eighteen years than any man alive. With the exception of certain old drivers who later cared for Hughes as medical aides during his lingering final madness, Chouinard knows he saw him the most. Noah Dietrich, Hughes' money man and a frustrated curmudgeon—close to him once—knew little more of his personal life than the standard cocktail-party myths. His New York-based attorney, Chester Davis, never saw him. Bill Gay, the harassed and desperate executive in charge of the communications center at the Romaine Street office in Los Angeles, listened to the Old Man's harangues and vituperative denouncements daily but didn't see him for years on end. Nadine Henley, his onetime personal secretary, busied herself in a corner office and had no contact with Hughes. Robert Maheu, who was to manage the enormous Hughes combine in Las Vegas before a bitter quarrel caused The Boss to fire him, admits that he never saw him. Hughes was also a phantom to the executives of Hughes Tool; TWA; Hughes Aircraft; RKO; the Medical Institute in Florida; the helicopter firm; television station KLAS in Las Vegas; Hughes Airwest; the brewery in Texas; the Xanadu Princess Hotel in the Bahamas; Archisystems, an architectural engineering branch; and the Sands, Frontier, Desert Inn, Landmark, Paradise Valley Country Club, and Silver Slipper casinos and hotels in Las Vegas.

Those around Hughes always suspected that he was elusive because he felt the lack of personal contact gave him a certain omnipotent presence, like the Wizard of Oz. He was never above sharing a box lunch with a mechanic or laborer, though he feared and distrusted executives. Chouinard was his daily personal contact with the outside world of women, other employees, his houses, and planes. For days on end during a crisis he'd call the detective every hour with orders and questions. How many times did Hughes actually meet with him? Too many.

With Chouinard's unique role came personal power in the jealousy-ridden Hughes hierarchy. As a shadowy "insider" some thought he knew what the Old Man was plotting. He liked the mystique and cultivated it. It was seldom true. For in the neurotic world of Howard Hughes there was only one insider. Chouinard's job was to expedite the Old Man's peculiar desires and frantic decisions of the given moment.

During those years between 1949 and 1968 when he was Howard Hughes' chief security agent Chouinard spent approximately $2 million. He hired 288 detectives and guards, nearly all of them college kids or Chouinard's relatives or relatives of relatives. The brighter ones became quite skillful. By official count he kept detailed case histories on 108 girls as well as unrecorded scores of files of casual encounters Hughes briefly thought he fancied as potential mistresses for his harem.

Operating under the name Mike Conrad, Chouinard was as unlikely a private detective as any of the amateurs he hired during those years. He was always bewildered when he read of "the wall of supersleuths" Hughes had built between himself and the outside world. *Life* once claimed they'd "do justice to the CIA." Now Chouinard realizes he was as infected as anyone in the Hughes personal organization by that rampant paranoia which came with working for this eccentric man, yet at the time the crazy pursuits and ludicrous misadventures—frenetically dictated by the maddest of all—seemed terribly important.

Chouinard's background was strikingly dissimilar to that of the Texas billionaire who was to turn him into a sleuth. In 1923, when a Houston judge awarded control of his deceased father's business to Howard Hughes at age nineteen, Gerald Chouinard won his own prize as the biggest baby of the year to be born in Lisbon, Maine.

The tiny southeast village (population approximately 380) was half "narrow-backed Yankees" and half "Canucks," anyone of French-Canadian ancestry. Each group felt superior to the other and had since the French and Indian Wars.

The lad's first love was workhorses, and he resolved to be a farmer for a time, then discovered the sea and settled on becoming a Maine coast fisherman. By the time he was eight—when Hughes was taking his first flying lessons at Clover Field in Santa Monica—Chouinard, too, had fixed on flying, after his father paid five dollars for him to fly in a barnstorming plane.

In 1937, a year after Hughes broke the coast-to-coast flight record and received the Harmon Trophy, Brother Brodeur, Cleres de St. Viatour, visited Lisbon looking for students for St. Joseph's College in Berthier, Quebec, Canada. The cost was $18 a month at a time the average factory worker in the town was making $17 a week. His parents went to the sugar bowl for their hard-saved cash and enrolled him, hoping that his ultimate destiny would be better than a hand in the local textile facory. St. Joseph's College proved to have been inspired by Dickens' *Oliver Twist* with a touch of the Marquis de Sade. It was a bilingual prep school of a sort where boys survived on peanut butter, beans, "shellac" (molasses), and a stern ritual of prayer. Those who didn't get bogged down in snowdrifts trying to escape during the brutal winters were encouraged to take vows. Chouinard settled on becoming a missionary after two visitors came to lecture on the starvation, paganism, bandit warfare, and general horrors of China. It sounded like a summer camp to him.

By 1940, when Hughes had bought control of TWA, Chouinard was a senior and a class oddity because he subscribed to *The New York Times,* a newspaper without comics. He was soon emotionally caught up in the European war and wrote home to say he was going to become an RAF pilot and the missionary stuff would have to wait. His father replied curtly that England could go to hell.

Chouinard returned to Lisbon soon after and—at the same time that Hughes was squiring the loveliest movie stars—discovered the curious merits of girls as well. He got a job as a Fuller Brush salesman and soon won the top-salesman award of the area, simply because he had the most relatives. He frittered all his money away on local lovelies.

At eighteen he took off for Boston, although one local warned him against even a visit. "Why do you wanna go to Boston for? Boston will never amount to anything. It's too far." His mission was to apply for the V-5 program at the Naval Officer Procurement Office. He went through the examination in a grand sweep until he hit the test for color blindness. He was told he could never expect to be a pilot or even a deck officer and was washed out. Crestfallen, he went to a local optometrist to verify the navy's finding. He noticed the doctor was using the same test book as the recruitment examiner had and, after the doctor agreed with the navy and then turned his back, Chouinard stole the test book and took off for Lisbon.

A month later he returned and passed the navy's color-blindness test. Told to stand by for orders, he got a job in a Portland, Maine, shipyard. Soon after he was in navy training at Williams College, where he decided to take it easy until the real thing—flying school—came along. Chouinard nearly washed out of training school but won the questionable and unofficial title of class prankster. He went on to Austin Peay State College in Clarksville, Tennessee, and completed pre-flight school at the University of Georgia. Then came regular navy flight primary training in Iowa. His penchant for stunt flying nearly grounded him but he sneaked through and stayed in service till the end of the war.

Soon after, he bought a surplus navy SNV trainer, had his license suspended for ten different FAA violations—the tenth being reckless flying—and purchased four more planes, which he lost either by cracking them up or because he was in various difficulties for violating rules.

Since 1948 Chouinard had been in Los Angeles, working as an insurance investigator for one year. It was monotonous, as his first and only love was flying. After the war he'd been drifting from one job to another and decided it was time to get married and settle down. But filing reports for insurance firms wasn't his idea of a happy future.

His dream was to make a single-engine solo flight around the world. If there was some way to get a plane, he reasoned, the rest would be easy. He started checking and found that Paul Mantz owned a modified North American P-51 "Mustang" fighter. He'd sealed the wings, souped it up, eliminated external tanks, taken off all excess weight. He'd raced it a few times but the ship, the fastest propeller plane around, now sat idle in his hangar at Lockheed in Burbank.

He met Mantz and, after negotiating a bit and outlining his idea, Mantz agreed to rent the plane at a reasonable rate if Chouinard would put up a $20,000 bond. The next major problem was clear: How to get the money? He needed a sponsor. He considered contacting oil companies, banks, various manufacturers, but decided it would all be too complicated. He was a novice promoter. What he needed was some dramatic gimmick that would bring immediate benefit to a sponsor while the flight was in progress. Where should he look? Hollywood, where magic things happened!

He was an amateur in such matters but started investigating which movie studio might be a possibility. Someone told him of *Joan of Arc,* a big-budget production just finished by Walter Wanger at RKO. It seemed to be in trouble, the movie buff explained, and might be able to use a crazy publicity stunt.

He managed through a friend in the wholesale fabric business to get an audience with an RKO publicity man, a sour and depressed former newspaperman, who obviously hated promoters. The RKO executive kept grunting as if he had gas pains somewhere behind his large cigar as he listened to Chouinard. Though he didn't reveal it, Chouinard's plan was to pull a Wrong-Way Corrigan act but with an added fillip. He'd set out for Paris but go off course and land in Stockholm. He'd then refuel, say he'd made a mistake, and announce that he was heading for Paris. Then he'd cut out across Russia, some three thousand miles, to Tehran. As the Cold War was in full flurry at the time he reasoned that such a mad dash would create worldwide press excitement, not to mention all sorts of diplomatic consternation. Since Communists were then shooting down any alien aircraft, he planned to fly low to avoid radar and, in his opinion, stood a good chance of making the run without incident. Russian peasants didn't have telephones, he reasoned, so they couldn't report his flight; neither did Russia have a propeller plane that could catch him. He'd also worked out a wildly romantic contingency plan in case his motor went out or he crashed.

He'd wear Russian peasant clothes under his flying suit and if he got lost or suffered engine failure, he'd ditch the plane and suit and make his way out of Russia posing as a deaf-mute.

But the Tehran leg of the spectacular trip was only the beginning, as he saw it. He'd fuel up and make a run over Red China from Calcutta to Formosa. There he envisioned being greeted with ticker-tape parades and worldwide fame. If the flight to Tehran weren't enough, surely by the time he got to Formosa he wouldn't have to cross the Pacific. He'd never have to check out another insurance claimant again!

He'd written General Claire Chennault in Washington, D.C., about the idea. (He still has his yellowed reply.) If Chennault thought Chouinard was crazy, his solemn interest didn't indicate it, although he tried to discourage him from flying over Communist China. He explained:

> In reply to the questions submitted in your letter of 5 February I suggest the following:
>
> 1. Avoid flight over Communist China Mainland. Recent reports indicate they have moved a number of MIG units to the South and Southwest. It has been known for some time that they have an effective radar interception net.
>
> 2. Plan your course from Calcutta to pass just South of Yülin Bay, Southwest tip of Hainan Island, thence to Pescadores Islands and to Taipei. If Taipei is closed in or too low for safety, land at Tainan—170 miles Southwest of Taipei. Tainan is CAT maintenance base and Chinese Air Force jet base. My men there will furnish you any assistance you may require if you show them this letter.
>
> 3. You should have landing permit for Taipei, alternate Tainan. Remember, Formosa is at war with Red China and strange airplanes are intercepted. Cable or write well in advance to Director, CAA, Taipei, requesting permission to land and take off—technical landing—on or about a specified date.

Again CAT at Taipei will assist you if we know approximate date your arrival. . . .

The RKO executive listened and kept chewing Tums as Chouinard talked. "We're over budget already," the RKO man hedged, "but I'll mention this to my boss." It was obviously a dismissal as he concluded with that show-business classic, "Don't call us, we'll call you."

Chouinard was despondent and ready to give up. Then some ten days later he received a call from the RKO man. "Go over to eighty-four eighty-four Sunset Boulevard and take the plans you showed me," he announced. "Someone wants to look at them. Be there at two o'clock sharp."

The address on Sunset Boulevard belonged to an unimpressive building. Chouinard was met by a bluff, pleasant man who shook hands and introduced himself as Walter Kane.

Kane motioned him into a rattan-furnished living room. A lean, tall fellow in an open white shirt sat quietly in an armchair. "This is Howard Hughes, Mr. Chouinard," Kane said easily.

While Hughes, who owned RKO, wasn't as famous a figure as he was to become later he still was impressive to Chouinard as a flyer. It was like meeting Lindbergh.

"Let's hear what you have in mind," Hughes said softly. "They told me a little about it and it sounds pretty risky to me."

Chouinard outlined his project again while Hughes sat with his long legs crossed, silently picking at his fingernails. Chouinard noticed that Hughes' brooding, dark eyes never looked at him directly and it bothered him. He believed that old wives' tale about not trusting a man who wouldn't look you in the eye.

"Even if I get as far as Tehran," Chouinard concluded, "it would create all kinds of excitement and be a real kick in the ass for Russia. They'd have to admit it . . . much as they'd hate to."

Hughes shook his head and chuckled dryly. "There's a damned good chance you'll get lost or have engine trouble. Why do you want to risk your life for something like this?"

Chouinard didn't have a very good answer. "I lead a pretty dull life," he said weakly. Hughes asked what he did and listened sympathetically as Chouinard told of his dull job. There was a long silence when he finished.

"I'll keep thinking about this, but meanwhile I need an investigator. How would you like to go to work for me?"

Chouinard couldn't imagine what he could do for Hughes as he knew little about actual detective work. He told him so. Hughes shrugged, dismissing his lack of background as unimportant. "I've got an ex-FBI man working for me now and I think he's screwing the hell out of me," Hughes replied. He continued playing with his long fingernails and staring at them, the longest nails Chouinard had ever seen on a man. "Why don't you go try to get a job with him?" Hughes continued. "You'll learn something and if you can find out what he's doing to screw me, you can take over as my security man."

Chouinard was disappointed as Hughes jotted down the man's name and address and handed it to him. He thanked him but said he was really interested in the flight, not in being a cop. Hughes stood up in a gesture of dismissal. "Well, think it over, and I'll keep thinking about backing the flight." It was the first of the hundreds of times Howard Hughes was to put a carrot in front of Chouinard's nose to lead him on.

Dejected, Chouinard walked out into the bright sunlight and headed for the nearest bar. After a few drinks the carrot Hughes had so casually tossed out lured him. If he went to work for Hughes' security man, he'd be able to push the round-the-world flight idea. If he didn't? Well, it seemed that this brief meeting would be the end of his dream.

He looked at the crumpled slip of paper with the security man's name on it, then headed back to work. He made a fast check on the Hughes detective through the Retail Credit Company, getting background on him, and a day later visited his office, explaining he was an insurance investigator from the firm with which the detective had a policy and wanted to bring his file up to date. In answer to Chouinard's questions, the detective calmly lied that all he really did was check credit, that there was no rough stuff and no reason to raise his rate.

They concluded the interview. "Gee, I'd like to go to work for you," Chouinard said.

"Give me your number. If we get busy, I may call you," the detective replied. "I could use a good interviewer."

A week or so later the detective called him to do a small job. Then another. Eventually Chouinard quit and went to work for him full time.

Chouinard had infiltrated and was now a Hughes spy.

A few months after he began working for Hughes' security man, Chouinard concluded that Hughes had been right. By deft padding the detective had overcharged Hughes some twenty thousand dollars. Chouinard reported it and Hughes grimly thanked him. Slowly Hughes began to call Chouinard more than his boss with requests. Partly this was due to the fact that the detective's wife would often tell Hughes her husband wasn't in. Hughes knew it wasn't true, and this infuriated him even more.

One day it all ended. Hughes refused to pay the twenty thousand dollars, fired the detective, and Chouinard found himself Hughes' private eye. Hughes insisted he select a name under which he would operate and Chouinard chose "Mike Conrad and Associates." Telephone operators found "Chouinard" difficult to understand anyway. He soon had a private detective's license and was working out of his Burbank home exclusively for Hughes with a guaranteed retainer, work or no work. He listened daily to the monotonous drone of the Old Man as he instructed him in the sly ways of sleuthing, how to keep down costs, the need for absolute and complete secrecy, and then, once again, how to keep down costs.

If Hughes thought he'd rid himself of his crooked employee, however, he was in for a surprise a few months later. The detective was a tough operator and literally caught the Old Man with his wrinkled pants down when he trapped him in a public toilet at the Flamingo Hotel in Las Vegas. He grabbed Hughes and threatened to pummel him unless he got the twenty thousand dollars. Hughes went out to the desk and arranged for immediate payment.

Slowly Chouinard's pattern of duties began to emerge as the Old Man's trust in his secrecy increased. Chouinard hired several investigators he'd met at his last job. Their major mission was Hughes' preoccupation of the moment—Communists. Chouinard's men investigated people Hughes thought might be Reds in the movie business. There were others who were attempting to blackmail the billionaire and some who were actually collecting. A few cases involved actresses and movie "discoveries" but these females were not as numerous as they were to become later. When they did appear Hughes always insisted Chouinard handle the case personally and talk to no one about it.

A real crime surfaced when a spare engine for Hughes' personal Lockheed Constellation disappeared at his aircraft plant in Culver City. Hughes was determined to solve the case and catch the culprits. He arranged for Chouinard to have complete security clearance to go anywhere in the plant. The new detective spent weeks desperately questioning scores of employees but got nowhere. Then, as was so often to happen, Hughes' interest ended overnight and he started Chouinard on a new project.

Hughes' former security man had always sneeringly called

Hughes "Henry" or "The Man" behind his back but "Howard" to his face. Chouinard had adopted this informality when he chatted with Hughes at first, but noticing that everyone else used "Mr. Hughes," he decided formality was more in order. A few times he timidly asked Hughes if he'd given any more thought to the round-the-world flight. "We'll talk about that some time when we're not so busy, Jeff. I haven't forgotten," Hughes would reply.

Sometimes Hughes' calls seemed nothing more than the rambling chats of a lonesome man. He seemed to have concluded that Chouinard was an ardent anti-Communist as a result of his plan to annoy the Russians. It was a major preoccupation with Hughes at the time, as Chouinard learned when they twice had long and fervid discussions on the Cold War.

Chouinard ardently agreed with Hughes' stand. He even proposed to go to Hong Kong to check on factories that were shipping goods in increasing amounts to the U.S. Chouinard suspected a great deal of it was made in Red China, where trade was banned, and was simply passing through Hong Kong. Hughes listened attentively and said, "Your hunch is probably right, or why else would Red China allow Hong Kong even to exist? But I don't want you to go personally as I need you here. Who could you suggest for the job?" Chouinard said he'd look around, but before he could make a suggestion Hughes had his own anti-Red program underway.

Hughes was furious about a movie being made in New Mexico, *Salt of the Earth,* which he claimed was straight Red propaganda. One of the "Hollywood Ten" fired by Hughes at RKO was involved. Now he had a plan ready to destroy the "domestic Commies" who were trying to foist this film on the American public.

He phoned Chouinard. "I want you to rent a plane, a small one in bad condition, and go down to where they're making this picture. Get an old air force surplus jacket and make friends with the crew. Act like a dissatisfied veteran who is a Left-winger of some sort." His voice was excited as he elaborated. Hughes would arrange to leak information to the New Mexico radicals that they were never going to get the film developed in any lab in the U.S. "Now the thing is, when you hear them talking about this you volunteer to fly the film down to Mexico without going through customs to get it developed. But instead fly it right back here to Hollywood. We'll just steal that trash!"

Chouinard felt there were a few holes in the idea, such as whether they'd hand over their valuable film to a complete stranger or believe he was what he claimed to be.

Hughes brushed such trivia aside as he continued with enthusiasm. "I'll tell you what! I'll arrange for you to pick up a plane at Phoenix. Go get some old clothes and that jacket and make a reservation to fly to Arizona. When you get ready to leave, call me from the airport."

Confused, Chouinard hung up. How was he supposed to launch himself on this crazy adventure within a few hours? Yet, in a way, the sheer foolish audacity of the idea fascinated him.

That afternoon he was at the airport ready to depart. He called the Old Man.

"Cancel until the next flight," Hughes ordered crisply.

He did, then called again. "Cancel until the next," Hughes repeated.

He called five times. The last time the Old Man said, "Forget the whole thing."

He never knew why. *Salt of the Earth* was never mentioned again.

CHAPTER 3

BUT HUGHES PERSISTED IN TRYING TO FIGHT COMMUNISM. One day he commented, "Jeff, I still wish we could do something. Why don't you turn your mind to thinking up something I could do?" He went on to elaborate on the need for everyone to fight back against the Reds.

Chouinard was more than ready to oblige but didn't know just how. By then he'd had a taste of the Old Man's love for romantic and elaborate intrigue so he set out to devise a plan. He supposed, too, he felt a bit guilty as he had little to do but assign college kids to their posts and draw nice pay checks.

He eventually worked out an elaborate plan titled "Ambrose: An Anti-Red Proposal" and sent it to Hughes at the Beverly Hills Hotel through a personal contact rather than through the staff. Aware of Hughes' concern with secrecy, he began:

"The reason for giving this to you this way is security, which you will understand after reading it. I suggest you tear it up and flush it down the toilet. Remembering our conversations on the Red Menace and the bleak outlook because of it, I have carefully worked out a plan that I think is feasible and could bring valuable results. It is an ambitious plan that should be carried out by the government or the CIA but it could be better done by you since it would depend upon absolute secrecy and not a single leak. With the government too many people would have to be in on it.

"You may have heard that when the wind is favorable, people in Taiwan fly helium balloons carrying propaganda messages over mainland China. My idea is to do the same thing over Russia. But not drop leaflets, as they would have no more effect than Radio Free Europe. Let's drop U. S. cigarettes with short freedom messages written on them or around them!

"1. Virginia tobacco is favored all over Europe.

"2. It is lightweight, especially if packaged in lightweight containers.

"3. American cigs are dirt cheap when you deduct the taxes.

"If somehow we can get them at cost, or even have them donated, this is where the government could help. But we would have to have some sort of cover to throw them off as to their real destination. Both the balloons and the cigs would be nonmetallic of course and radar would not pick them up. They would be launched at night. The entire operation could be done by Portuguese fishermen. The Portuguese are anti-Red. They fish in large sailing vessels far from their homeland. For instance, they can stay off Newfoundland for months and months, so it wouldn't be difficult for them to sail to the North Sea. The crew could be selected by the clergy in Portugal for their reliability. These ships could actually fish and carry fish but have false bottoms for the balloons and cigs, which could be jettisoned in case they were stopped by a Russian submarine. The balloons could be made to burst after reaching a predetermined altitude."

He sat back for a response. If the Old Man wanted him to think big, he mused, he'd certainly done it.

Days later Hughes called. "About Ambrose, have you discussed it with anyone?" he asked in a hushed voice. "Any experts? How many people know?"

"No one, not even my wife."

"Good! Don't break it to a single soul until we have a chance to talk about it. The first problem is who would head this project? Who would have enough know-how? I haven't been feeling well at all but as soon as I'm a bit better we'll have to meet somewhere. I'm trying out a new plane, an

Electra. Maybe you could come along—there's no better place to think straight than when you're flying. Be ready."

Chouinard eagerly agreed.

"In the meantime don't neglect your other projects," he added. "What I mean is put Ambrose on the shelf completely until we can talk about it more. I think you have one hell of an idea there!"

Chouinard hung up, quite taken with his own ingenuity as a global plotter.

A week went by and he got word that Hughes was going to leave the Beverly Hills Hotel to try out the new Lockheed Electra. He assumed the Old Man would want him along to talk about Ambrose, as he'd mentioned.

He sat by. The office had a driver parked near the bungalow behind the Beverly Hills Hotel where Hughes was staying. The driver sat there for five days. Chouinard waited daily for the call to join Hughes.

The car was still at the curb when Hughes called for another driver to come to the hotel garage one morning, meet him, and take him to Burbank without Chouinard. He flew that day to Santa Fe to view a house he thought he might lease. He never mentioned Ambrose again.

CHAPTER

4

CHOUINARD WAS TO SUSPECT THAT THE OLD MAN'S INTEREST in communism was a psychological reaction to Hughes' similar mode of operation. For beyond secrecy, intrigue, and suspicion of being surrounded by unknown enemies, he ran his entire empire much as the "cell" concept of communism. He constantly compartmentalized and separated one unit and one executive from the other. He feared a buildup of anyone's power that might lead to an in-group that could make trouble. The nerve center of the Hughes organization was an unlikely Hollywood citadel formally known as "Operations" but referred to by employees simply as "Romaine." The headquarters originated through a typical Hughes business foulup. Hughes had obtained rights to a color-processing method for movies and had gone to Canada in the 1920's to shoot an outdoor movie. He was wildly enthused and built the structure at 7000 Romaine Street as the first color-processing plant. Each floor—carefully fireproofed—would house labs where Hughes would develop film for studios. His dream fell apart overnight when Technicolor made a breakthrough and developed a color process that was much cheaper. The Hughes method was abandoned.

Soon after, the ground floor was leased to a brewery. Its major highlight and a tragedy of that period was a fountain, still there, that flowed free beer for a time. So many bums gathered with tin cups each day that the brewery cut it off.

Hughes himself had an office on the second floor, lore has it, but no one recalls ever seeing him in the building. Today it's dusty and filled with his souvenirs, discarded furniture, a spare tire from his racing plane that is fifty years old, a decaying wooden model of his flying boat, his Collier trophy. The building itself is an aging, one-block-long rectangular structure with locked doors, a decaying exterior.

Romaine was a paradox of confused, twitching nerve endings as befitted the Old Man's nervous system. The rules for anyone entering were elaborate, and varied with the importance of the unwanted guest. The bottom floor was quite empty except for a few mysterious offices where "secret assignments" were in progress, storage rooms, and the office of the aged "Professor," a mysterious oldster who worked out the Old Man's movie schedules, clipped newspapers, and brooded a great deal.

The Professor was a remarkable person, a retired bachelor schoolteacher from Chouinard's home state of Maine. He'd been hired when he was in his seventies. This short, thin, spry Yankee loved to have someone ask him to show off his agility. He'd jump up and leap over a chair. He'd been known to send his friends a picture of himself in sunglasses and a long black hippie wig, holding a guitar. He was still at Romaine in his late eighties and, spry as ever, was providing the only sunshine that building probably ever had. Though he must have picked up loads of juicy tidbits, he was secretive. Out of mutual respect and friendship, Chouinard never questioned him. But once the Professor couldn't resist showing Chouinard a stack of addressed envelopes containing regular checks for friends, some former employees, and ex-girlfriends of Hughes. There were eighty-seven. The Professor was outraged. There was no retirement program for employees at Romaine.

There were two others at Romaine that Chouinard respected and liked, Lee Merrin and Kay Glenn. Merrin by that time had been with Hughes for over thirty years and had handled the payroll for Hughes Aircraft when the company was in one room leased from Lockheed. He had been hired as a cinematographer when Hughes was thinking of cornering the film-developing business with his new color process.

Merrin is the only close Hughes associate Chouinard knows who never fell out of favor or trust. Though he had not seen Hughes in several years he was handling the most important personal money matters, such as payoffs or infrequent charities that Hughes wanted kept confidential. The millions and millions of dollars that came from the tool company in Houston would go directly to Merrin, who would then pass the money on to Romaine for all of Hughes' personal expenses. While it cost Hughes about $2 million a year to live, much of it was deductible.

Lee Merrin was to remain Hughes' most trusted employee through all the years. There were many other financial advisors but the keystone of the structure remained the man who'd started with Hughes in one room at Lockheed when he was building his racing plane.

The endless dollars from Hughes Tool filtered through him to seed all the other enterprises. Chouinard recalls the time when he was being paid in cash until it could be decided what business entity he'd be under. Merrin would methodically take out a key and open a drawer in his desk. Neatly stacked were piles of paper money up to $1,000 bills. All were new and untouched by human hands as the Old Man had instructed. If payoffs were made to troublemakers, the money came from here.

Chouinard himself would take the cash, which made up his combined payroll for the security men, and go to a bank teller, where he'd count it out to be put in a checking account. The teller, a precise and proper gentleman, was always intrigued as the detective counted out the thousands, commenting laconically, "My girls really worked hard last week."

Among the moneymen of Wall Street tales emerged constantly of Hughes' intrigues, most of them false. He reportedly had powerful politicians in his hand. He was so deeply immersed in the worldwide machinations of the CIA that he could call the shots with other governments. His billions had translated themselves into a power so devastating that there was no controlling his wishes.

If so, it didn't show. He had an endless running fight with the Internal Revenue Service year after year. Decades later, at the very end of his life, the IRS was reportedly ready to declare him legally dead before the news came of his actual death en route from Mexico. Even then the IRS ordered fingerprints taken from the corpse to compare with those in the FBI file. He was wanted, as the old Western movie signs went, "Dead or Alive."

One year Attorney General Robert Kennedy complained bitterly to the press of a multimillionaire who had paid only $500 in income tax the previous year. Merrin told Chouinard that Kennedy was referring to Hughes.

Another staffer at Romaine Chouinard was to befriend was Kay G. Glenn, a Mormon who had been a General's aide during World War II in New Guinea. He was hired as a secretary at $75 a week at about the same time as Chouinard. (Today he is second in command under Bill Gay, the president of Summa Corporation.)

Bill Gay was a thin young Mormon with light, crew-cut hair who favored conservative suits and affected a cold and distant manner. He was bland, meticulous, neat, and a dry conversationalist. He was, in a word, a complete contrast to Chouinard, who was given to practical jokes, socializing, and a friendly drink. They grated on one another. Chouinard, for example, found the perfect device to escape a long and tedious detailed discussion of his weekly expenses when he visited Gay's office. The detective would light a large cigar and Gay, sniffing and gasping, would soon dismiss him.

Nadine Henley, who had been Hughes' secretary for years, was married to a man who worked at Hughes Aircraft. She had an attractive personality, was pleasant and efficient. She had built her own role by daring to take more authority as the years passed. She enjoyed a drink and dressed handsomely, with good jewelry.

Within this little hierarchy there were endless daily conferences as the team constantly pondered decisions that had to be made, wondering how to get word to the Old Man and get an answer back in time.

While most of the personnel in the office and in the driver pool were Mormon, there was no strict religious rivalry or prejudice involved. The non-Mormons or "Gentiles" among the employees were often annoyed at the holier-than-thou attitude of the Mormon majority but attributed this to their membership in the Romaine Street "elite" rather than the Mormon Church.

The infiltration of Mormons into the Hughes organization, continuing until they finally took over, had begun years before, in an odd way. The head of Hughes' staff had been an Irish Catholic, now dead.

One Christmas Eve, Hughes received word that a TWA plane had crashed in South America. Aides doubt that he was aware either that it was his birthday or Christmas Eve, for he immediately started calling staff members to get more details and to start checking what points of international law were involved in the crash.

He called his Irish executive, who was not at home. Then another employee and another. A few answered his summons but were apparently brimming over with Christmas cheer. He was in a panic as the phone was, even then, his contact to the outside world.

Nadine Henley was also unavailable, but at the bottom of the list he did at last reach her male secretary, a youth just out of college in Utah, Bill Gay.

"How come you're not drunk or at a party?" Hughes asked angrily.

Young Gay was on the alert. "Sir, my religion doesn't allow me to drink."

Hughes grunted. "Yeah? What religion is that?"

"The Latter-Day Saints."

The day after Christmas the Old Man called Nadine. "This Latter-Day Saints thing? What is it?" Nadine explained it was another name for Mormons.

"Let's start hiring a staff of Mormons here then," he ordered. "They'll be available when I need them and they don't drink."

He paused a moment. "Hell, they'll even be better than Catholics. They don't have to go to Mass on Sunday like those Irish."

Gay's ascendancy had begun. He religiously—if you'll forgive the expression—followed the Old Man's edict as openings occurred until nearly the entire office staff was made up of Mormons who didn't drink or smoke, swear or take coffee.

The second floor at Romaine Street was furnished more than a decade before Chouinard went to work for Hughes and was quite luxurious, with thick rugs, walnut desks, paneling. Glenn, Gay, and Henley all had offices here. Howard Lundeen had an office where he handled real estate and accounting. An elaborate twenty-four-hour communications system with huge boards was always fully manned as well as filled with all the complex card systems dear to insurance companies and government bureaus. Even the looniest crackpot call had to be carefully recorded, summarized, and filed here in a proper place. If it was "made work," no one would admit it.

Hughes himself had helped plan this elaborate complex of record keeping, electronic gadgetry, and militant work schedules. Everything was geared to his dreaded calls to dictate a memo, chew ass, or make an inquiry as to messages. Every request for him by a caller was carefully chronicled as to time, the name of the caller, the nature of his business, the caller's apparent mood, how frequently he'd called before, and any random conclusions the operator had to add.

If The Boss didn't want to reply, which was usual, he'd give careful orders on how to handle the matter, what to say, and even in what tone of voice. All this was duly filed each day.

Hughes was firmly against tape recorders. He'd call in messages that Mormon clerks would write out in shorthand and then type. Often he'd ramble on for an hour, outlining detailed instructions on some bit of trivia. He peppered these memos frequently with four-letter words and oaths when he was angry. This gave some of the more religious clerks fits, and they'd privately substitute a more proper terminology as a code to avoid the nasty expressions.

A variety of rules were rigidly enforced at Romaine. Don't smoke; don't drink; don't eat garlic, onions, Roquefort cheese; don't go to movies, sporting events, or mix in large crowds. Don't, above all, have a cold or a bronchial infection. As with the military, never ask why, just do what you are told.

Hughes feared the idea of any strangers ever entering the Romaine Street building. Every noon hot food came from the aircraft-company kitchens so the staff wouldn't go to restaurants to eat. A bucket was lowered from the second floor by a fishline and short rod through a window to pick up all packages or mail. Chouinard was especially annoyed at first when they'd throw his pay check to him from the second-floor window and it would blow down the street while he chased it. It was during a period when Chouinard was suspected of being a germ carrier.

Rules for car-pool drivers, made up of more clean-cut Mormon youths who would often take aspiring actresses to expensive spots for dinner after lessons—always with a parent or agent as a chaperone—included that one must talk only of sports, show biz, or the weather and never become friendly. They had other routine chores: picking up newspapers, ice cream, mail, meeting VIP's at the airport.

It was still another rule that one driver out for dinner with a Hughes' starlet must never recognize another driver with a starlet in the same restaurant. With four or five girls—all Hughes' protégées but all supposedly unaware of the others—dining in the same restaurant such as Chasen's, Perino's, or the Beverly Hills Hotel dining room—this could be an awkward and unlikely farce. Particularly when the starlets knew the other Hughes drivers with the Hughes girls seated nearby. But the Old Man liked to believe he was fooling everyone and keeping his doings compartmentalized. The drivers, however, spent a great deal of time with the various starlets, picked them up for their lessons, waited for them, and developed personal friendships. Hughes was always wary of their chummy closeness to the girls.

Chouinard had nothing to do with the motor pool but would hear constantly of the Old Man checking up to be sure there was no hanky-panky. Disaster struck once when a beautiful and talented actress—a Mormon girl—announced that she was planning to get married. That was bad enough, but she was marrying one of the Mormon drivers, Miles, who'd been hauling her about. Vera Miles went on to build a career on her own.

The Boss was in a rage. The Mormons were in hysteria as the Old Man called several times a day to denounce this executive then that one for the slovenly lack of vigilance and control. Then an edict came down from on high. The Old Man had decided the answer was to hire homosexual drivers.

It was a thorny task finding candidates, particularly in those days before Gay Lib. Likely prospects would be sought out and called in for an interview. Then they'd be questioned hopefully. "Are you a homosexual?" Naturally, their reply was always no. The interviewer who prompted them and told them to say they were homosexuals was taking a chance as they were likely to say they were gay just to get the job—then turn out not to be! Another driver-actress romance was too much even to contemplate.

Eventually, a few homosexuals were put to work. They were assigned to particularly suspect girls who seemed to show an inkling for any quick romance. It wasn't long before there was a new problem. Two of the drivers were picked up in Santa Monica soliciting vice squad cops. Wheels had to grind to hush it all up. The Old Man reluctantly agreed that homosexuals weren't the answer. Chouinard always suspected he secretly envied those storied Eastern potentates who could castrate at will and then turn their harem over to fat eunuchs.

CHAPTER 5

IF THE OLD MAN BROODED OVER THE SEXUALITY OF THE young drivers, he was equally apprehensive about Chouinard's guards. He was most emphatic about employees' histories and wanted a report on each of them. He was always fearful that they'd pick up too much knowledge of his activities and wanted constantly to know how Chouinard could compartmentalize their jobs so one wouldn't know what the other was doing. It was impossible, but at the beginning the detective did try. Hughes would listen to Chouinard's logistics on guard insulation and pick on some minor detail with elaborate ideas of how to improve it. From these talks Chouinard came to understand how frustrated top executives of Hughes' vast empire must feel.

The most minute item would suddenly focus his whole attention: on which corner a guard was to stand, northwest or southeast; how a car was to park at sunset. Days would be taken up in game plans about such nonsense. Everything would stop while the Hughes tunnel-vision took over. In retrospect, considering the nature of Chouinard's humble tasks, he had a right to be annoyed, but not disgusted. If Hughes was involved with the important decisions on aircraft or missile production, one can only wonder what administrative horrors must have been created.

Hughes queried Chouinard constantly about the moral caliber of his men. He kept repeating his old bromides, warning that "what they'll do for you they'll do to you" and demanding that they all be "true blue." Use people who aren't too clever but are just smart enough to do the job, Hughes cautioned.

Chouinard agreed in principle but for more practical reasons. He had decided early not to hire professional private eyes. In Hollywood they could be bought by the bushel basket and were all problems automatically. To begin with they were generally a sleazy lot looking only for the main chance to loot a client or even blackmail someone if they could. Those with good reputations were anxious to keep them and, if they made a mistake, would often lie to cover themselves. With someone like Hughes—with his multiple sources of information—Chouinard could easily have found himself caught in the middle. He knew that if he wasn't told what was really going on and the Old Man found out, all hell could break loose.

Ex-policemen were another problem. Most were usually just former patrolmen or the like and knew nothing of detective work, although uniformly they claimed they did. If they were older and retired, they usually resented being told what to do by someone younger and refused to try to learn. Hence, Chouinard decided early in the game that his best chance was to hire friends or friends of friends or relatives so he'd have at least some idea of their background and character.

A few moonlighting policemen were also effective, though good ones were often hard to find.

Even with his best efforts to build an effective team there were constant foulups. When these occurred Chouinard could either lie or simply admit the error and hope not to be replaced. For pragmatic reasons Chouinard usually told the Old Man the truth when his men goofed. Hughes was ordinarily quite sympathetic.

Another perennial problem was keeping constant close contact with someone in the police department. Chouinard had to make instant checks on license numbers, for example. The routine at the time required that you drive downtown to the Department of Motor Vehicles and pay a quarter to get a name and address on a license number. The detective seldom had time for this. Hughes would spot someone in an auto and call Chouinard, wanting to know immediately who owned the car. The way to get it quickly was to call a secret number the police and FBI had at the DMV. You'd simply call, rattle off the license number, and identify yourself as Sergeant Smith at the Hollenbeck Division or the like. In a few moments you'd be given the information. But other private detectives and various credit investigators would soon get the number, and it had to be changed constantly. You needed someone on the inside to keep you informed of the new numbers.

Chouinard was afraid his detectives were serious disappointments to the Old Man. Most were clean-cut college types wearing t-shirts and Levi's. They were more given to chewing bubble gum, eating junk food, and napping under trees than being sinister and mysterious.

Once, Walter Kane, the Old Man's crony, was having some important people over when Hughes would be there and asked couldn't Chouinard find a few guards who really looked "bodyguardy." Chouinard couldn't fill Kane's order out of his own ranks so he asked a friend, Andy Cuoco—an

Italian barber—to lend a hand. Andy is black-haired, tough-looking, and tall. That evening he wore the kind of suit gangsters do in the movies, and Walter was delighted when he saw him standing menacingly out front. "You don't have to tell me where you got that fellow!" he beamed. "When I shook hands with him I knew he was from either the FBI or the CIA." Hughes never cared about his personal safety, and Chouinard is sure the idea of having a personal bodyguard never occurred to him at the time any more than the prospect of being kidnapped or done in by a crackpot assassin.

Chouinard's turnover of personnel was constant. He'd have to juggle hours all the time so his team could go to school. Also, he was under endless pressure by Romaine to keep expenses down. When things were quiet he had to lay off men. Some would return when he needed them but many drifted off to more secure jobs. He tried to pay them $2 an hour which, for the time, was fairly high. Those who stayed eventually earned as much as $3.50 an hour. It was a reasonable wage for a college kid although rather low for an organization such as Hughes'.

Each new man was a concern to Chouinard. One wiretapper he hired from time to time kept the detective constantly worried. The man made up in crass bravery what he lacked in subtle trickery. The wiretapper owned a truck that was a duplicate of a telephone-company truck and would simply climb poles and tap into a line in broad daylight. While Chouinard feared his methods, he was one of the best men available until he was caught later in Mexico trying to bug John Wayne's apartment and got the apartment of the governor of a Mexican state by mistake.

Chouinard's final bewilderment with this brazen operator came when he attended a Cub Scout meeting with his young son at St. Charles Church in the San Fernando Valley. Standing in front of the assembly was the wiretapper in full

Boy Scout uniform, handing out good citizenship awards to the youths!

At first Chouinard vowed always to tell Hughes the truth. But Hughes' unique orders and demands created endless temptations to lie to him. The Old Man was accustomed to this and had developed a number of ruses to put a novice employee in his place. He'd never accuse anyone openly of fibbing but would simply push him to the wall.

Soon after Chouinard started to work for Hughes he got a call one rainy night at about 2 A.M. "How are you? I want you to go to a pay phone and call me back. I have something important to discuss."

He sat on the edge of the bed and listened to the raindrops fall in the gloom. To hell with it, he thought. He waited about fifteen minutes and called the Old Man back from his bedroom.

"Are you at a pay phone?" Hughes asked immediately.

Chouinard lied and said he was.

"What's the number there? I'll call you right back."

Chouinard stammered and then explained that some vandals had scratched out the number on the dial.

"Then go to another phone and call me back again," Hughes replied.

Chouinard pulled on a raincoat, dashed out, and drove to a phone booth. Hughes repeated his request and the detective sat in the booth until Hughes called back and got down to the problem at hand.

This stunt, Chouinard was to learn later, was one of The Boss's favorites to get a reading on his staff's reliability.

Once Harry Cohn borrowed some sets from RKO, Hughes' studio, to use on the Columbia lot. When Hughes found out he was furious. Later on, a director came across Hughes at the Flamingo in Las Vegas and casually asked him if he knew where he could find a trained crow to steal for an upcoming production. "Go see Harry Cohn. He'll know," Hughes grumbled.

Though the Old Man preached and demanded honesty from those around him he felt it was a luxury for a man of his wealth. Long after Chouinard had gone to work for him he'd been ordered to tap in on one girl's phone, he recalls, and overheard a talk between the girl and Hughes.

Hughes was complaining of some business dealings that had turned sour. "Well, Howard," she admonished him, "if you'd just tell the truth all the time you wouldn't have such problems."

"Listen, honey," he replied, "a guy in my position couldn't live with the truth. I wouldn't last a month if I told the truth."

He walked the tightrope between complete truth and bitter cynicism. One of the things that made him furious was the belief held by some that a man of his power could do as he pleased at any time. Once he was grumbling to Chouinard about someone who'd said he could do anything dishonest—even have people killed—and get away with it if he wished.

"It's just the opposite," Hughes explained. "The more money you have the less you can afford to be crooked. If you do, you have to involve someone else and then there's no end to the payoff. How could I live if I had to worry about dozens of people I knew had something on me?"

Yet one could never tell when the Old Man was operating by pure whim, whether he had one of his plans afoot and your part of the mission was one piece in a great jigsaw puzzle he'd invented, or if he was just being mean. His motivation seemed always to operate from a shifting platform, and the detective now supposes in all truth Hughes didn't know himself much of the time. Hughes' telephone, as already mentioned, was like a king's scepter. Without it by his side to keep control over his vast domain he became immediately frantic. With it and with his serfs at the other end he must have felt omnipotent and in complete control. He could dictate, pass out favors, and create panic.

Typically, he called one of his executives, Perry Lieber, at home one night. The line was busy. He tried several times more, becoming increasingly more frantic. The next morning a telephone man arrived at the Lieber house with orders to install another phone in Lieber's bedroom. Lieber was never told what the number was. Only Hughes knew.

The Old Man swore constantly, particularly over the phone. Face to face with someone he tended to be much the gentleman unless outraged by something. Chouinard would often be talking with him on the phone and Hughes would be, as usual with the detective, polite and soft-spoken. Then Chouinard would hear another phone ring in the background and he'd ask the detective to hold the wire. Hughes would pick up the other phone and Chouinard could hear him launch into a tirade using every known vulgarity and profanity. Then he'd return to the conversation with Chouinard and continue, softly discussing the sleuthing job at hand.

Much as he liked the Mormons for their stability, Hughes took a fiendish delight in shocking them at Romaine. Chouinard would often get calls relayed to him through the communications desk, and the operators would start deciphering instructions the Old Man had ordered passed on. He could tell by the hesitant pauses that the caller was censoring his notes to eliminate the crudities he'd had to listen to from The Boss. They hated it but had to take it.

Most of the executives were no better off. He liked to awaken them occasionally in the middle of the night with a few shocking expletives to clear the sleepy sand from their eyes. He preferred to phone during these late hours for several reasons. First, he simply never operated by the clock, preferring his own natural time; he'd doze for four hours, then go back to work for ten or twelve. Second, he seemed to feel more secure when he called at three in the morning knowing whoever he wanted to contact was at home. Chouinard thinks Hughes also suspected he could get the quick truth from a man he awakened by surprise from a deep sleep.

The detective always suspected that a prime reason Hughes hired him, kept him on, and refused to hire an ex-FBI man or a big-name investigator was that Hughes could play his own vicarious role as an amateur private eye through Chouinard. They both knew Chouinard was an amateur and untrained when he began. A really competent security officer could have given quick and logical reasons why not to pursue any of the Old Man's schemes. That would have ruined half the fun.

This may have been the underlying reason Hughes showed Chouinard more respect than he did Bill Gay or others. He never cursed the detective and was, ordinarily, uniformly polite. This was, Chouinard thinks, because Chouinard was in Hughes' mind his playmate in the fascinating game of Supersleuth. Chouinard knows Hughes must have gone out at night and studied the premises on cases they were involved in much of the time. He usually seemed to know the terrain better than Chouinard did.

"What do you think of this?" he'd start. "We put a man near the big elm tree on the corner and a surveillance car down half a block around the corner on Canon Drive. That will cover the side entrance and front. Then in the back . . ." He'd go on to detail time schedules, weather problems, and the like. The detective knew Hughes had drawn a map and spent several hours working it all out.

Seldom would it make any sense. If the subject didn't spot Hughes' men, the local police certainly would and get suspicious. But Chouinard always agreed with some suggestions Hughes made. He'd follow the plan for a few nights in case Hughes might cruise by to check, then revert to some simple routine.

Typical of the Hughes penchant for overplanning and turning a simple task into a vast complexity was the time he called Chouinard from Las Vegas. He'd seen a pretty girl with her family in one of the hotels. He'd sent a bellboy to try to get her name but it had been impossible and she was with her parents now en route to Los Angeles on the train.

At that time the train always stopped in Pasadena before its final destination, the Los Angeles terminal. "I want you to board the train at Pasadena," Hughes began. "Just flash your wallet to the conductor and tell him you're an FBI man and that you're looking for some missing secret government papers. Then start going through the train until you see an unusually pretty girl with her parents." He went on to give Chouinard a glowing description of his new find.

"Go up to them and tell them you're with the FBI and ask to look at their luggage and identification. Get their names and address and then we'll be all set."

Chouinard knew by then that simply to point out to Hughes that he could be in all kinds of trouble by falsely identifying himself as an FBI agent was hopeless. Nor was it wise to mention that the family might refuse to cooperate with him. When the Hughes blood was up, all things were possible. They'd just have hours of discussion, with Hughes' will prevailing.

Chouinard merely said he'd follow through. He got on the train in Pasadena, spotted the girl, followed her and her family to their auto, and got the license number. He called Hughes back with her name and address in a few hours.

"Did you follow my plan?" Hughes asked.

"Yes, sir."

"I knew it would work like a goddamned charm!" he chortled.

The detective recalls a case he's sure was one of the happiest in Hughes' career as an amateur detective. He'd been assigned by The Boss to tail a woman staying at the Beverly

Hills Hotel. Hughes was in the hotel and could watch his men and the subject from the window. He called Chouinard when the woman drove up and gave him a blow-by-blow account of what was happening. "There are two cars in front of the subject, who is now parking at the side. Your man is back at the corner waiting for a light. The subject has turned in. Your man has turned left. Another of your men has picked up the subject to follow her into the hotel. . . ." He was delighted with the whole operation and congratulated the detective on what a professional "team" he was running. Sometimes Hughes seemed more intrigued by the chase than the prize.

Once he became suddenly interested in a Las Vegas showgirl whose boyfriend was a Las Vegas police officer. Chouinard was ordered to tail him. Chasing a cop on his own turf was a sure way to find trouble, Chouinard knew, but the Old Man was eager, ordering the detective to call him every hour with a progress report. Getting such calls through to Los Angeles took most of his time in the early 1950's, but within a day Chouinard had discovered the cop was a family man and the showgirl wasn't aware of it. Hughes delightedly gave her the news that her boyfriend was married and heard her break into tears on the phone. Once he'd destroyed the romance, he lost all interest in her and never called her again.

If Chouinard had trouble with the Old Man and his elaborate plans that he so despised, he often had just as much trouble with Romaine and his "team" of amateur college boys and relatives. They often wanted to play detective as well and use disguises, code names, and electronic gadgets of some exotic variety. Ordinarily Bill Gay talked of little else but how to keep expenses down. But all those clever electronic gadgets intrigued Gay beyond belief.

The bugging of girls in the Hughes camp was always done at residences Hughes legally owned or leased. Some of it may have reached into a gray area of civil rights. Chouinard doesn't know. He remembers setting up a bugging radio in one apartment to establish that one girl was probably cheating on Hughes. It was more than he'd reckoned for as he picked up the grunts, groans, and sex talk of the girl having intercourse with a boyfriend.

Chouinard gladly turned the tape over to Bill Gay, who presumably always had to forward such material to the Old Man. But Gay was never satisfied with the clarity of the evidence and questioned the detective's competence constantly. At one point Maheu sent two men who had allegedly found the microphone in the eye of the eagle at the American Embassy in Moscow and were supposedly on their way to plant bugs for Trujillo in the Dominican Republic. They were reputed to be the best but turned out to be incompetent washouts despite their fine equipment.

The now defunct *Collier's* magazine created a crisis with Gay about then when it ran an article displaying all the latest electronics gear, which was James Bond stuff. Such items as the notorious bug in the olive in a martini glass sounded wonderfully exciting but seldom worked unless conditions were ideal. For example, a crowded bar with glasses tinkling and background talk wiped out any advantage. If one was in a hotel with steel reinforcement, for another example, he couldn't pick up talk outside the building. There was a parabolic plate that was about two and a half feet in diameter that could be set up on a tripod and pick up conversations at a distance. But who was going to walk into a hotel lobby or dining room and assemble it without being noticed? Bill Gay, however, thought the security men should get all the gadgets and damn the expense.

They did have transmitters that sent out a bleep and could be clamped on the bumper of an auto in case a detective lost someone he was following. With a radio direction finder one could locate this target car. Yet even this was only good in some spots, such as the San Fernando Valley or an open area.

In the city, with buildings framed on steel girders, it was easy to lose the prey. At one point Chouinard used a small plane he had, a little side-by-side Taylorcraft of about 85-horsepower, that could cruise slowly behind an auto, but it was not practical.

Chouinard's team resorted to the more primitive sort of thing at night. One trick was to break out the red glass of a tail light in the car they were planning to follow. The bright white light was a splendid guide a block or so away. Sometimes their prey was stopped by a black-and-white patrol car who would politely tell their victim the problem. It wasn't exactly the James Bond sort of thing, but it worked and did keep down expenses in a way. And—as they were almost always following girls of a naive and trusting nature—it never seemed to occur to the girls to wonder why or how that tail light had been broken. They'd usually mention it to Hughes, who would then pay to get it repaired, knowing by experience what had happened.

CHAPTER 6

IN RETROSPECT IT'S EASY TO LAUGH OR TO BE FILLED WITH scorn at the activities of Howard Hughes. He was everything that gossip and lore claimed. His personality contained contradictions so massive they make a jumble out of any effort to define him. He was an enigma in a paradox in an absurdity in a riddle. Yet when he started out, he seems to have been a man of singular purpose.

His early days were sprinkled with flashes of brilliance. As a boy he built one of the first radio stations in Texas. When his father died Hughes was eighteen. He persuaded a judge to declare him of legal age, bought out his relatives, and took over Hughes Tool Company. With the endless profits from the Hughes patented oil drill he went to Hollywood and made *Hell's Angels,* now a film classic. In 1935 he built his H-1 racer which set a world speed record of 325 mph. In 1938 he flew around the world in 91 hours, 14 minutes, and broke the previous record by four days.

His bitterness years later toward the press and public who laughed at his flying boat and dubbed it "The Spruce Goose" was justified. No one now recalls that Nazi U-boats were wiping out ships at a staggering rate at the beginning of World War II. He set out to build a huge flying troop transport that could have saved thousands of lives. He made it of wood because metal was in short supply. By the time the eight-engine Goliath (as big as today's C5A) was completed the war was over. Life had moved on; it was easy to sneer.

Among his more fascinating contradictions was how he consistently sought out places that offered the most potential for congeniality, crowds, gaudy fun, and witty conversation and then, with no explanation whatsoever, cut himself off from any contact. Why, aides often wondered, didn't he go to those hundreds of lonely and isolated places where he'd be left alone?

His avid reading and concern with science and aviation left them similarly puzzled. Why did he never visit Cal Tech, MIT, or consult with scientists or aviation experts? He showed no interest in any of them except for their products.

The social scene meant nothing to him. He completely avoided his Texas relatives. His tendency seemed to be to gravitate to those places where the most superficial and vulgar people congregate and then avoid them at all cost.

The security and secretiveness surrounding Hughes was so taken for granted that no one ever questioned it. Later, when germ phobia had become the prime motivating factor for his self-imposed prison and solitary confinement, the reason was obvious. But before that time he had no real fear of kidnappers, reporters, people trying to borrow money, ask for his autograph, interest him in investments, or even kill him.

His major concern was running into all those old girls. God knows how many there were, but they were likely to be found in places he liked to frequent such as Miami, Palm Springs, Las Vegas, and other spas. He lived, Chouinard knows, in constant dread of meeting them. This was, of course, because of the ungracious way he'd discarded most of them. Most he'd simply dropped cold, cutting off their funds and moving on, leaving them furious and filled with hate. He dreaded the time when he'd be cornered by any of them, particularly in public, and face a terrible scene. It explained why his regular routes in and out of buildings and hotels were the service entrances and fire escapes.

Chouinard recalls a major foulup in a Miami hotel. The Boss had word that one of his old girls was nearby. Arrangements were made with the management for him to use fire doors. Things went well for a few days, and then when he tried his regular fire door he found it locked. Worse still, Chouinard's guard wasn't inside standing on duty to take care of such a crisis. There was nothing to do but go through the lobby.

It couldn't have been worse. The discarded girlfriend came out of one elevator just as Hughes was scurrying for another. "Howard!" she cried, causing everyone in the lobby to turn.

He could do nothing but stand trapped. Happily, she greeted him effusively, and he promised to call her that evening. Then he went to his suite in a rage and called Chouinard. After yelling about lax security for a few minutes, however, he suddenly and inexplicably began to laugh over the whole debacle and hung up.

There were those who contended his later phobia had roots in reality. Chouinard could never believe it. His lungs were injured in his 1946 air crash, this version went, hence he lived in fear of chronic bronchial infection. He lived in fear all right. But the detective wonders at the easy diagnosis. Some said he was shy about his appearance after three plane crashes had mangled his nose and cheeks. If he was mangled, it was hardly discernible.

If one cannot understand the reason for Hughes' fears, neither can he understand why Las Vegas held the fascination for him that it did. Hughes had absolute contempt for the underworld. The hoods were wary of him and those at the top knew how he felt about them. The detective recalls the time before Hughes "invaded" Las Vegas when he mulled over the idea of starting an aircraft factory there. He even bought land across from the Flamingo Hotel as the site. Gang leaders were in a frenzy when word got out. The one thing they didn't want in Las Vegas—particularly on the lavish Strip—was a factory. They wanted high rollers, not a working-class town.

When Hughes heard of their consternation he seemed delighted. But Hughes Aircraft officials convinced him that the proposed plant would be too remote from other facilities.

Frank Sinatra was another of the Old Man's pet hates. His dislike started years ago when Sinatra and Ava Gardner were married. Ava had been an old girlfriend and she and Hughes remained close friends. When Sinatra supposedly pummeled Ava she came running to Hughes. He arranged for an attorney and had the divorce papers delivered to Sinatra.

Hughes waited to get a vengeance of sorts years later when he moved into Las Vegas and started buying up hotels. One of them was the Sands, where Sinatra, Dean Martin, and Sammy Davis, Jr., performed regularly. Sinatra felt he had built the place and that it was his, even if Hughes did own it.

One afternoon Chouinard went to visit Walter Kane, Hughes' companion and employee, who was in the hospital. Walter was wide-eyed. "You know who was just here to see me? Frank Sinatra! He wants me to talk to Howard. He said that if Howard would buy Sinatra's shares in Cal-Neva, he and Dean Martin and Sammy Davis, Jr., will sign a contract and appear at the Sands as often and as long as Howard wants."

At the time Sinatra was under pressure from the state of Nevada to divest himself of his Cal-Neva Lodge interests, the gambling casino at Lake Tahoe, because of reputed connections with a top Chicago Mafia boss, the late Sam Giancana.

The word was relayed to Hughes. There was no immediate answer. Chouinard is sure Hughes knew of Sinatra's desperation and enjoyed the whole idea of not giving a fast rejection. It was more fun to let him stew and hope.

Then at the last moment Hughes sent word that he wouldn't consider it. "I don't want any part of Sinatra," he said.

The result was evident in all the news stories of Sinatra running amok in the Sands. Apparently he got drunk and went berserk after his hopes had been built up. He drove a golf cart into the lobby and started breaking glass windows, yelling, "I built this goddamned place and I'm going to tear it down."

Sinatra was a feared celebrity in Las Vegas. But one pit boss solved the matter. He punched Sinatra in the mouth, knocking some teeth out and settling the incident. Old Black and Blue Eyes was flown to New York to have his teeth replaced.

CHAPTER 7

WALTER KANE WAS PERHAPS THE CLOSEST THING HUGHES had to a friend in the years before his increasing illness. And Howard Hughes was the closest thing Kane had to an enemy! Walter was the constant butt of Hughes' cruel jokes, his whipping boy, the subject of endless scorn and sarcasm.

Kane had sat silently in his apartment throughout that first meeting when Chouinard had tried to sell the Old Man his round-the-world flight idea. The next time the detective heard from Kane he was installed in a paneled office at RKO and seemed not to connect Chouinard with the first meeting.

"Mike Conrad?" he asked, using the pseudonym in a blustering voice when Chouinard answered his phone. "Get over here. I have an assignment for you." Knowing Kane was calling for Hughes, Chouinard drove hurriedly over the hill from Burbank to the studio.

He was asked to wait a considerable length of time, then ushered in. Kane was all ceremony and pomp, his chest out, his voice loud and authoritative. The assignment was a piece of trivia, and the detective wondered why Kane couldn't have simply told it to him over the phone. A week or so later he understood how desperate Kane was to be respected and have some authority.

One day Hughes called and asked Chouinard to come to Walter's apartment on Sunset Strip, which was a favorite hangout for the Old Man at the time. The conversation that followed left no doubt that Walter's bluster a week before was simply his way of trying to recapture some sense of dignity.

They were discussing a minor project Hughes wanted to get underway. Hughes sat in a rattan chair, wearing a white shirt and baggy tweed pants. As he outlined his plans Walter tried several times to interrupt with suggestions.

Hughes would cut him short. "You cut that crap! You haven't any brains and you should know it," he'd say. "Keep your goddamned mouth shut."

It was embarrassing, and Chouinard was caught in the middle. Yet after that he always felt more comfortable around Walter and grew to like him and sympathize with him in his awkward and humiliating role.

Hughes knew Walter's weaknesses and took a constant sadistic pleasure in torturing him. One of his favorite tricks was to insist that Walter fly with him on some secret mission. Walter was not a man to court danger. Hughes would take off on the flight and head for some remote place. He'd purposely carry a short supply of gas and point out to Walter the low gauge. Then, as Walter knew nothing about flying, he'd cut the throttle, causing the motor to cough, and watch as Walter turned white, green, and gray.

Another of his juvenile jokes was to put Walter in a bind and see how he could squirm out of it. Once they flew to

Arrowhead in a small plane. They landed, checked into a hotel, and went for a stroll in the village. Hughes spotted a pretty girl.

"Walter, I want you to find out who she is. Break the ice with her and give her the old pitch about a movie contract. I'll go back to the hotel and wait for you."

Kane went trailing off after the girl. Hughes jumped into a taxi, went to the airport, and flew back to Los Angeles.

Late that night Kane made it back by hitching a ride with some strangers. He called Hughes, quaking with suppressed anger. "Why do you do things like that to me, Howard?" he asked. "You left me stranded."

The Old Man laughed mirthlessly. "I figured you'd get to know that girl better if I left you and you had to ride back to town with her." He then went on to berate Kane when he found out Walter hadn't managed to make contact.

Walter's official function was as a middleman to sign girls to contracts once they'd been discovered. His routine was to arrange for a meeting with a girl's agent, if she had one, at his apartment. It would be a farcical little sketch. The agents all knew Kane's role and what the going rate was for a Hughes starlet, the standard $175 a week. The agent and Kane would quibble while the girl sat transfixed. They discussed possible starring roles a year or two in the future and clauses that would jump the salary to astronomical sums. Then they'd settle on the $175 and make the usual arrangements for various lessons. The girl would find herself in an apartment building such as the Westside Manor, where Chouinard's men would put her under the surveillance given each Hughes starlet.

Hughes also used Kane's apartment for assignations. It was understood that if Hughes arrived with a girl, Kane was to disappear after a few quick pleasantries. Sometimes Kane would go to the Beverly Hills Hotel, check in, and stay for several days, fearful of calling his own apartment to see if Hughes was still there.

Kane had come to the Hughes camp from a background of vaudeville. He'd worked as an agent with one of the Marx Brothers, Zeppo. He was an ideal man for Hughes' needs. He was familiar with the whole starlet market in Hollywood and an intimate pal of Walter Winchell's. Johnny Meyers was Hughes' go-between with the ladies and also organized parties for politicians and top-ranking military acquaintances. But Kane knew Hollywood girls by the score. He was put on the Hughes payroll at five hundred dollars a week and expenses.

If Walter was a man of broad acquaintance, he was not one to worry over fine details. Chouinard recalls being stunned one day when he asked Kane, who had been married to actress Lynn Bari, if his former wife hadn't been born and raised in Connecticut.

"I don't know," Kane shrugged.

"What do you mean?" the detective asked. "You were married to her."

"Well, I don't know. I just never asked her."

In 1960 Bari was to describe Kane to Chouinard's wife when they met at a party as "a great charmer but really something else to live with."

Kane was Hughes' constant companion on the little adventures. Once the billionaire decided to land his converted B-23 bomber on the small private airstrip on Catalina Island, which he knew was closed to all private planes in those days. After landing, he leaped out and turned to Kane. "Stay here," he ordered. "I have to make a fast run into Avalon."

The field manager told Hughes as he started to depart that he was in violation of rules and should leave immediately.

Hughes shrugged. "I don't know anything about it. That guy over by the plane is the one to talk to." Hughes hurried off while Walter tried to argue with officials for an hour about something he didn't understand.

Kane once mentioned that he sometimes yearned for the old days. He'd heard about the parties aboard Hughes' three-hundred-foot *Southern Cross*. Not long after, Hughes called Kane to tell him to dig out his yachting clothes, they were off for Newport for some sailing. Walter dressed meticulously and drove with Hughes to the landing. Hughes had rented a tiny eight-foot sailboat for children, not really big enough for two.

Walter allowed as how he'd wait on the dock. Hughes insisted. For several hours they sailed the tiny craft around the harbor, Hughes at the tiller and Kane clutching desperately to the sides. He never mentioned the good old days to Hughes again.

Even with such harassment from the billionaire, the balding, stout Kane still managed to lead a sybaritic way of life. He was always broke by the weekly payday, having dined in splendor at LaRue's, Chasen's, or simply having ordered a dinner catered in. He was fond of fine silk shirts and ties and ordered his suits from Sy Devore's, a show-biz favorite. There was a flamboyant dignity to him when he was in full sartorial glory, which was enhanced by his assured manner and his need to be the bon vivant.

Kane enjoyed this good life and knew how to live it well with his host of friends and pretty companions. He admired tough people and mimicked their guttural street talk. He drank carefully or not at all. The regular visitors to his apartment on Sunset Boulevard included Walter Winchell, Jack Dempsey, Rudy Vallee; he often bragged that he was godfather to the child of the head of Columbia Studios, Harry Cohn.

If the Old Man misused Walter in many ways, he did use Kane's clothes most effectively. He was constantly stealing Walter's jackets, shirts, and pants. Some early pictures of Hughes show him in sport jackets with sleeves too short or shirts that don't fit. They were usually Walter's. The Boss couldn't take the time or effort to go to a store to buy clothes and would pick up what was around anywhere for any occasion. To add to Kane's frustration, Hughes never admitted those thefts, and when Kane complained, Hughes just shrugged and changed the subject.

Once Kane rebelled. It had been raining and Hughes went to Kane's closet and took a vicuna overcoat. It was Walter's prize possession and he was furious. He kept nagging the Old Man to return it. Hughes denied knowing anything about it, but Kane wouldn't give up. He complained to everyone who'd listen about the coat. He'd whine to Hughes every time he appeared. Still the Old Man claimed he knew nothing about such nonsense.

Finally Kane went to Romaine Street and started a campaign to be reimbursed. It became a cause célèbre. In desperation and to get rid of the nuisance of listening to Walter, the Romaine brass at last gave him the money to buy a new vicuna coat.

Hughes would often ask people to Kane's apartment to settle some business involving movies. They had a secret system. As the business talk progressed, Hughes would excuse himself and go to the bathroom. He'd scribble a note to Kane, then return. Kane would then excuse himself and go to the bathroom, read Hughes' note, and write a reply. They always felt they were outwitting the negotiators with this stunt.

Hughes' efforts to confuse and frighten Kane sometimes took a truly wry and amusing turn. One Sunday afternoon they were at the Kane apartment with identical Swedish twins someone had discovered. The two blond girls were exact duplicates down to their red painted toenails. They'd settled down in bathing suits on the sundeck overlooking the city and were sipping Tom Collinses when Hughes motioned to Walter to follow him inside.

"Now remember," he said, pointing. "That one's Mary and the other one is Mona. I don't give a damn about Mary. She's yours. But don't fool around with Mona."

Walter studied the situation and agreed, returning to the sundeck. A bit later, as Walter sat rubbing suntan lotion on Mary's back, Hughes called for him to come back to the living room.

"You son of a bitch," he whispered. "I told you to leave Mona alone."

"But Howard, I can't tell them apart. I thought I had Mary."

Hughes was in a mock rage. "You dumb bastard! Any stupid asshole can tell one's ugly and the other's beautiful."

Kane returned to the sundeck muttering.

Hughes was sometimes shy, even in his most urgent demands. When the information he wanted seemed too embarrassing even for him he'd have Walter Kane relay the orders to Chouinard.

In 1954 Walter called. He was officious. "There's an actress The Boss likes. He wants you to find out if her bust is natural or if she's had one of those operations. She's got whoppers, I understand."

"Are you serious?"

"You bet your ass I am! Howard wants to know right away."

"How the hell am I going to do something like that?" Chouinard pleaded.

He could almost see Walter shrug at the other end of the line.

"You'll find a way." He gave Chouinard the name and hung up.

The detective wondered what to do. He thought maybe the best thing was to stall and hope the Old Man would forget. Yet that wasn't likely. He wondered if he could just go up to her, grab, and find out. But he wasn't anxious to go to jail on attempted rape.

Then he remembered a friend of his wife's who'd said she'd wanted one of those silicone operations. He called her and asked if she'd ever checked out the doctors who did them. "Not all," she said. "But I know the names of the ones who do most of them in Hollywood."

"I want to hire you to do something for me," he said.

The plan was simplicity itself. She hit gold on the first doctor, a questionable physician, who managed somehow to advertise his specialty.

She visited him for an estimate. "I certainly did like the job you did on my girlfriend," she said, giving the name.

"Oh yes," he replied. "That turned out beautifully, didn't it." He went on to describe for her the details of the girl's silicone treatments.

The day came when Hughes simply withdrew from his camaraderie with Walter Kane. There was no incident, no phone call, no explanation. Hughes was sick; he was gone. Kane's private line to The Boss never rang. Kane brooded, wondered, discussed with friends what might have angered Howard. He became desperate as the months passed and he heard tales that Romaine was about to take him off the payroll.

Chouinard visited him frequently. On one occasion he obviously purposely left a medium-sized black notebook on the coffee table. "I'll go fix a drink," he explained, glancing significantly at the notebook, and disappeared.

Chouinard knew he was supposed to look at it privately. Listed alphabetically were several hundred names of girls Hughes had been interested in at some time. Chouinard browsed through the names, many of which were familiar. Then he stopped in amazement. His own wife was listed! In retrospect Chouinard is sure Kane had no idea. He just wanted Chouinard to report to Romaine brass what sensitive information he had so they'd try not to drop him from the payroll.

Chouinard was startled but not shocked to find his wife's name. She'd been in several movies. He told her when he went home. She laughed, recalling a movie she'd been in starring Tony Martin, *Two Tickets to Broadway.* It was a bit part, but five of the loveliest girls had been asked to be photographed at the studio of Christy Shepherd, Hughes' official photographer. Only one of them, Mara Corday, had gone on to greater things as an actress. His wife had heard nothing more. But they mused over the way Hughes reached out everywhere.

Chouinard was not too amazed. Long before, he'd browsed through the files of girls at Romaine that were kept in the message center. There were hundreds of photos.

Kane continued to wait for Hughes to call. Two friends pulled a prank one night. They got the number of the private Hughes phone and called. One rang while the other sat with Kane. It had been years since the phone had rung. Kane turned white, then went to the phone. A voice inquired for Edith and apologized for a wrong number. Hope gone, Kane slumped back.

Today Kane is about eighty years of age. He is in charge of entertainment for the Hughes hotels in Las Vegas. A huge sign in front of the Desert Inn declares "Walter Kane Presents" and lists the featured star. Walter is in his element, and his new role has revitalized him.

Chouinard was with him one day when he was dealing with the singer Wayne Newton, who has a long-term contract involving millions. Chouinard sat amused as Walter told Wayne and his agent off, explaining to them where they stood. It was the old Walter, who'd been so pompous and gruff with him years before in his paneled office at RKO. Newton and his agent didn't recognize this Walter and listened solemnly as he raged and shouted.

CHAPTER 8

WHEN CHOUINARD THINKS OF THOSE SCORES OF ANONYMOUS females who moved through the peripatetic Hughes harem over the years he finds it impossible to view them as desirable vixens, seductive sirens, or simple sexpots. To him they were annoying subjects—the enemy!—and represented only the problems they brought.

Some can't conceive of Hughes carrying on with this assorted crew. They agree it's a foolish thing to say but Hughes "just didn't seem the type!" It's easier to imagine Herbert Hoover in his high collar and BVD's running amok in a brothel.

There's a need to make a clear distinction between these playmates and the stars Hughes escorted in public. During the 1930's and 1940's he was seen with an endless parade of stars such as Katharine Hepburn, Lana Turner, Ava Gardner, Olivia de Havilland, Terry Moore, Ida Lupino, and Jean Harlow. Within the Hughes organization it was understood that none of these were serious romantic interests or affairs of any consequence even though Ginger Rogers said he proposed to her and Terry Moore claims she and Hughes were married at sea and he later destroyed the ship's log record of the event. Jane Russell was strictly a business investment when she emerged as a star in *The Outlaw* in 1943 and remained so.

The harem was housed at various apartments and rented homes on the west side of Los Angeles, usually selected by a real estate agent. In addition there were the homes Hughes was continually planning to lease for himself and Jean Peters when he was living at Rancho Santa Fe. He made detailed explorations regularly and then stalled. When a likely selection was made Hughes followed a rigid routine. He sent a covering memo on the matter but regularly added new requirements by phone.

Before Hughes himself decided to move back to Los Angeles, Jean Peters expressed a desire to visit Los Angeles more often and attend ballets and operas. Hughes was determined she'd select her own house and not stay at a hotel. Most houses under consideration had to be new and never occupied before. Security men had to stand guard for three months so any germs left by workmen would have died. Then Jean Peters was allowed to look over the premises. Hughes' agent found some ten houses. Guards would stand in front of three to five different homes at a given time. If there was any mishap, such as an owner getting on the property, the house was dropped as a likely candidate. Meanwhile Virginia Tremaine, the real estate agent, had to try to keep the owner interested until an actual lease was signed. When, after some months, Jean Peters did arrive to look over the houses, she took the first one she was shown in Trousdale Estates.

Even though Hughes didn't own these houses, Chouinard's men had to be careful when they approached. A car with a guard should never drive to the house on the right-hand side, Hughes explained, but stay in the middle of the road. This, he went on, would eliminate the hazard of picking up leaves and trash on the tires. Hughes always viewed gutters with the same dread he had of flies, sore throats, and dirty money, even before his illness.

Chouinard complained once. "It's pretty damned dangerous driving up those curving roads in the middle of the road at night."

There was a moment's silence. "Not if your men are well trained," Hughes replied.

Once at the residence the auto was to be parked twelve feet above or below the property line that bisected the road, at least two feet from the curb. Though this led to some parking tickets, they were paid and the practice continued.

Now a cat-and-mouse game began. It would have cost a great deal of money to lease these houses and leave them empty until Hughes or Jean Peters occupied one of them. So the game was to leave the owners hanging on the lease until the Hughes contingent was actually ready to move. While the realtor stalled the owner as long as possible men stood guard over property that Hughes neither owned nor leased.

This led to some quaint situations. If the house was empty, the owner would sometimes arrive; guards were instructed not to allow him to enter. Most owners would simply go away from their houses shaking their heads in bewilderment. But now and again one would blow the whistle. "This is the United States of America and this is my house," cried one indignant property owner the guards had to turn away. "Who are you and how do you think you can keep me out of my own house?"

The guards were naturally under instructions to give no clue to Hughes' involvement. They'd just instruct such people to call the realtor, who'd explain. The realtor would stall, not knowing what was going on and, if things got too hot, the Hughes forces would either complete the lease or disappear. It didn't work with a particular indignant citizen. He went to the police. Chouinard called Romaine and was told to disappear. Romaine then went to work on the matter with a police commissioner, and authorities managed to convince the owner that he was "involved in something much bigger than you understand. . . ."

Carrying out the letter of the eccentric Hughes' law required unusual measures at times.

Once, a massive meter reader arrived at a house where a small man was standing guard. The guard explained that it was private property and the meter reader couldn't step past the curb. The meter reader wasn't to be put off so easily. He cited the fact that the city owned an eighteen-inch square around the meter and, as the meter was only fourteen inches from the curb, it was city property and the owner had no jurisdiction.

The guard showed a flair for brilliance and started debating the distance, claiming it was more than eighteen inches. He sent another guard for a yardstick and whispered instructions to him to call Chouinard and find out what to do. Chouinard immediately called Romaine.

The guard returned, they measured, and the meter reader grinned in triumph. "I'm warning you that you'd better call your boss before you do that," the guard threatened.

The meter reader must have agreed that something was indeed whacky because he went to call. By then Romaine had contacted a man on the water and power commission and wheels had turned. The meter reader was told just to forget the whole matter. He went away muttering about international spies and how a man couldn't do an honest day's work anymore.

Chouinard, meanwhile, thought he'd confuse the issue when he explained to his newly hired guard after the incident that the real client for the house was Cecil B. De Mille. He went home and told his wife. "De Mille's been dead for a year," she replied.

If property owners and service people felt annoyed and confused when they encountered the guards, Chouinard sometimes felt just as silly. One terrible moment came when his men were guarding five or six houses at the same time. His father was standing by at the huge, empty Xavier Cugat house in Brentwood, his father-in-law had charge of another mansion in Trousdale Estates, where Nixon had once bought a home, and others were at a woman singer's rambling ranch house in Brentwood, which was already under lease.

Chouinard was short of men and he'd secretly eliminated the midnight-to-eight shifts at the singer's house. While he had no idea when it might "get hot," that is, when occupancy seemed close, he guessed this house would be the last to be chosen. He had stopped for inspection and everything seemed all right. Yet in the back of his mind he knew he was not following Hughes' instructions to the letter and he felt something was amiss.

Dawn came like thunder when Bill Gay called him one morning. "Pull your man off and be there yourself," he said. "The Boss is coming by to look at the place today."

Chouinard hurried over. The college kid on duty at eight that morning was in front of the empty house, lounging against the mailbox.

"Is everything okay?" Chouinard asked, still having a queasy feeling about something he couldn't pin down.

The youth shrugged.

"As far as I know. The only thing this morning was that I had to chase the pool man away. He got here at eight and said he was an hour later than usual and had to get back to clean the pool."

Electric lights flashed in Chouinard's head as in a cartoon-strip balloon. That was it! He ran back to the pool behind the house. It was immaculate—yet the house had been empty for seventeen weeks! The damned pool man had been coming in at seven once a week before his man went on duty and had been cleaning the pool!

He knew by then how the Hughes mind worked. The Old Man would be sure to see it and know someone had been on the property. Feeling like a fool, he spent the next half hour rushing about throwing dirt and leaves in the water. He looked at his final achievement with an artist's eye. It was filthy, a dirty brown with shreds of leaves floating about. The thought flashed through his mind, "What am I doing here anyway?"

He waited around all day. The Boss never showed up. Not, in fact, ever. Six months later he got word that the lease had been canceled and he could remove his guards.

This rule of not breaking a lease until Hughes personally ordered it led to some bizarre situations. One of the most expensive adventures came when the Old Man leased a house in Palm Springs, used it a few days one winter, and then departed. He left orders to leave the coolers on, as he'd be right back.

The staff stood by for some seven years awaiting word to end the lease. It came at last. Hughes' aides went to check the house. The evaporative coolers had run on and on through the years and all the plaster from the ceiling and walls had fallen and crumbled on the floors. Palm Springs is usually dry, but sometime during each year the humidity goes up. That, coupled with the coolers, had been too much for what was now a shell of a house.

Houses weren't Hughes' only problem. One day in 1961 Chouinard was informed that the Old Man had decided to buy a boat. The news sent cold tingles down his back. He'd once talked to an old fellow from Maine, Captain Flynn, who'd been skipper of Howard Hughes' ship when Hughes was only twenty-one. It was the three-hundred-foot *Southern Cross,* the biggest yacht in the world at the time, bought sight unseen from an English lord. When Hughes first saw it he exclaimed, "My God, it's big!" Once, when Lee Merrin had business to transact with Captain Flynn while the boat was docked at the Santa Barbara pier, Merrin arrived at night and asked someone where he could find the craft. It was looming above him as he stood unaware next to it assuming it was a commercial ship of some kind.

Hughes sold it later to a Swedish steel magnate and it eventually ended up as a ferry ship for troops in the South Pacific during World War II, carrying a crew of ninety! Captain Flynn, the old Maine captain, told Chouinard it had been one of the oddest experiences of his adventurous life as a skipper. He'd run Hughes' yacht from New York to Boston, to Miami, through the Panama Canal to San Pedro, back to New Orleans, constantly, always at the urgent orders of young Hughes, who somehow never caught up with it or organized the big group that was always going to board the boat for a long, festive cruise. The old captain was at sea almost constantly, stopping at a port just to pick up supplies and rush on to the next port. Only a few girls ever made it aboard.

Captain Flynn ruminated, "He was always after them young girls. He'd call me and say I was to pick one up in California or New York or someplace. By the time I got there she was always gone."

Now Chouinard had visions of a massive ship of the same sort with Hughes demanding dozens of guards at dockside, others on deck. He was sure he'd be faced with terrible intrigues involving various girls being sent aboard.

He was delighted when it turned out to be only a tiny thirty-five-foot cruiser. Apparently Jean Peters had mentioned she'd like to go boating. Mr. Evans, the dealer, was ecstatic when he contacted Chouinard. "Mr. Hughes called me personally," Evans explained, "and wants to buy the boat even though he's never seen it." Chouinard sighed and looked at the man with sympathy. Evans explained that he'd been instructed to show it to no one else until Mr. Hughes arrived.

The pattern was the same as that used for the houses. Hughes put a twenty-four-hour guard on the boat and issued orders to Evans. It was not even to be washed down with a hose. No one was allowed aboard. The grime and salt began to collect, but Mr. Evans was calm about the whole affair. Mr. Hughes, he told Chouinard, had called him twice personally.

Time went on. The rainy season came. Mr. Evans had never received a cent. Mr. Evans asked if he could close a window because the rain must be raising havoc with the cabin.

Absolutely not.

Could Evans go aboard and see what damage had been done? Nope.

It was eight months since the Old Man's first phone call. He had still never come to see the boat.

Evans eventually threatened to sue for his ruined, weather-beaten, salt-encrusted wreck with the mildewed interior and sodden inside deck. Romaine asked him to estimate how much repair would cost. It was nearly the price of a new boat.

The last Chouinard heard, one of the Mormons was complaining about how everyone took advantage of Mr. Hughes just because he was wealthy.

Some shrewd operators learned that Romaine could not act on its own but needed Hughes' personal approval on a variety of petty matters and took advantage of it. One of the more calculated rejections of Romaine's touted power came when a homosexual dress designer who had been on the regular payroll at five hundred dollars a week was told that he was fired.

The designer had been hired originally to create ideas for TWA stewardesses' uniforms, but his work had been rejected as too frilly. He'd stayed on to design clothes for a few of Hughes' girlfriends from time to time, but the Romaine brass in their endless effort to prune expenses felt he was a waste of money.

The designer just shrugged at the pink slip. "Howard Hughes hired me and only Howard Hughes can fire me," he announced. "The day he calls me and tells me I'll leave." He continued on the payroll, knowing the Old Man was in isolation in Bel Air by then and would never call.

CHAPTER

ANIMALS WERE A NEVER-ENDING HAZARD BOTH TO HUGHES and to the security operations. For Hughes they were like Mother's Day, Van Gogh paintings, or small children: He was unaware of their existence until they suddenly thwarted his plans or emerged to cause some form of confusion.

At one point during Hughes' heyday Chouinard had surveillance on five houses and apartments where various girls were in different stages of metamorphosis for their ultimate destiny. He had scrounged every existing relative of his, and their friends, for guard duty, as he needed a total of thirty-six for eight-hour shifts in addition to routine functions at other locales.

At four one morning Hughes called him in a stage of desperation. "Nancy!" he cried. "Do you know Nancy?" Chouinard hurriedly checked his case list in the stand beside his bed. Nancy was about nineteen, blond, interested in a singing career, and had been recruited somewhere out of the Midwest by one of Hughes' unknown procurers. She was living alone in an apartment in Brentwood, being coached by a singing tutor, had no upsetting phone calls according to the tape records, no boyfriends and, from apartment and trash searches during her absences, no correspondence that might cause problems. She was a singularly pleasant case from his standpoint.

"Yeah," he replied. "She has a good record."

"She's got a goddamned animal in there," Hughes went on. "The worst thing you've ever seen. Maybe it's an anteater or some fucking thing. How did it get there?"

"I don't know, Mr. Hughes." It's remarkable to Chouinard to think of it now, but he was terribly upset that his men had allowed this woman to somehow sneak some kind of animal—like an anteater!—into the apartment. Though they had regularly checked the premises, they had failed to report it.

"I want it out of there. I don't care how you do it, get rid of it!" Hughes yelled. "I was over there and the whole goddamned place is probably filled with all kinds of tropical diseases!!!"

The next morning they mounted an operation early. The girl's singing instructor called and told her she had to have her lesson early as a relative had taken sick and the instructor had to leave town. A driver and car arrived for her by nine and she was out of the way. Chouinard didn't know what he would encounter. He'd gone to a pet shop and bought a large wire mesh cage and brought leather gloves. He even had a pound of hamburger meat with a pacifier mixed into it in case he was really desperate.

They unlocked the front door. The living room was tidy and neat. In the bedroom the bed was unmade. The culprit was in the kitchen nibbling contentedly, in a Del Monte tomato carton, on greens and grain: a small brown and white guinea pig.

"Get rid of it," Hughes had said. Chouinard imagined the aftermath. The girl would be tearful and immediately call Hughes. He, full of fake sympathy and remorse, would call Chouinard to launch a search of the neighborhood with his short-staffed crew, saying he'd do everything to find it. Chouinard's men looked at the little critter's sharp teeth and worked out a ruse. Hurriedly, they chipped a hole with ragged edges through the kitchen door. From all signs, the girl was no trained biologist. She'd think, they hoped, that the animal had gnawed his way out.

That was exactly what happened. She called Hughes in tears. Her guinea pig had eaten a hole in the door and run away. They mounted a fake hunt so she could see it, and found nothing. Hughes promised to get her another pet. Chouinard doesn't know if he ever did. The guinea pig? One of the guards took it home for his kids.

During later days, in the 1960's, when Hughes had holed in at the château in Bel Air they faced more animal crises. A neighbor had a Great Dane that was always on the prowl. The guards panicked at the sight of it.

The Hughes forces were going through the fearful days of the TWA lawsuit, and the ultimate fear was that a process server would make his way into the Hughes bedroom. Each night Chouinard had a man stationed in an auto on a steep slope in the driveway, another on the side of the house, and still another in a maid's room to watch the far side of the house.

One night a chugging Volkswagen carrying a young couple, probably from nearby UCLA, made its way up the hill. The couple parked and began to embrace. Their progress was rapid and, because a Volks is a small car, they were soon out, the girl was spread across the fender, and they were at it.

The Great Dane appeared, raising all hell barking and howling. But the couple went on, seemingly oblivious to everything but their own passions. A guard rushed down, sure that a process server had arrived at last. He watched as the couple went on with their lovemaking while the dog, a few feet behind them, was awakening the whole neighborhood.

Then the girl saw the dog. They jumped and separated, scrambling for the car. Pulling up his trousers, the boy started signaling to the girl in deaf-mute sign language and she answered with her hands. They jumped into the auto and drove off.

Chouinard recalls one girl they'd moved into the Beverly Hills Hotel. They'd scared off her boyfriend, and she was upset and lonely. Hughes allowed her to get a French poodle, then a week later instructed Walter Kane to take it away from her. Kane did, explaining the hotel wouldn't allow dogs. She was in tears and immediately called Hughes to tell of her plight.

Hughes was outraged.

"Why that dirty old son of a bitch! I'll get your dog back. If he does that again, I'll fire the bastard," Hughes told her. "He must be getting senile." Kane returned the dog. But Hughes couldn't abide the beast, and a few weeks later it disappeared permanently.

Chouinard had his own run-in with another of those ubiquitous French poodles, the marauders of Beverly Hills, when he entered a girl's apartment in Coldwater Canyon to install a listening device one day when she was out. The dog was in the kitchen barking and howling. Chouinard foolishly opened the door and it rushed out and bit his hand. He cursed the animal but decided he couldn't steal it without orders.

Then he had more trouble with the animal world. There was a box of candy on a table in the living room, and he'd sampled it as he sat waiting for the bugger to finish the job. It was a foolish thing to do he realized after he'd eaten five or six pieces, but they did taste good. He turned the box over to see what they were and discovered he'd been eating chocolate-covered ants! It was some kind of gag, he decided, but he was sure the girl would miss the five or six pieces. He called around to find where such exotica was sold. He had to rush to Jurgensen's in Beverly Hills, buy a box, and return to carefully replace the missing chocolates.

The same girl was to cause a new commotion later, after they'd picked up her vicious French poodle. She wouldn't give up. She found a stray police dog. Hughes apparently saw another opportunity to be a hero, for he called the detective with orders to kidnap the dog.

French poodles were one thing but a big police dog another. Chouinard told Jim Boone, then a youth of nineteen, of the project. He was one of his best men and would walk through fire for him, Chouinard knew. (Today Jim owns an aircraft-parts business in Burbank.)

A few nights later there was a knock on his door. Jim had the dog in the back of his car. Chouinard called Hughes to report another mission completed. "Okay," Hughes said. "Treat him well and keep him. Feed him decently but don't go buying steaks or things like that. Whatever it costs charge to the office."

Chouinard really didn't want the dog around the place but there was nothing else to do. He started charging the office forty-five dollars a month to take care of the beast. Weeks went by and Hughes made no mention of returning the dog. Apparently the girl had displeased him in some way and it was increasingly obvious he had forgotten all about the animal as well as her. Chouinard talked with his aunt, who had a nursery in North Hollywood, and she agreed to keep it. "Don't lose it," he warned. "I may have to take it back at any time." Within a few days the dog had run away.

He waited anxiously for the call from Hughes saying he

wanted the dog back, but luckily it never came. He kept billing the office for the forty-five dollars a month, however, for several years because he was afraid if he stopped Hughes would somehow discover the dog was gone.

The major animal crisis, however, was to come when Jean Peters took in a battle-scarred tomcat with a missing ear when she was practically a recluse with Hughes in Bel Air. She went out each day to feed it. One day it disappeared.

She told Hughes of her loss and he was on the phone to Romaine immediately. "Call Jeff and tell him to get every man he can and start hunting for this cat," he ordered. "I want a progress report every hour. There's not much I can do for her anymore and I want to do this little thing."

Finding a cat in overgrown, woody Bel Air was like seeking the proverbial needle in the haystack. But Chouinard set out with three men, all he could muster on a moment's notice, to start searching. By late afternoon Hughes was in one of his rages as the hourly reports showed no results.

"Goddamn it, I don't care if you have to fly the best animal trapper in Africa over here to hunt for it," he said. "Find that cat or you're all fired!"

The next two days were spent in hysteria as the Romaine crew did little else but fret about the cat and their jobs. As usual Hughes turned his wrath on them rather than Chouinard for some curious reason, although they had nothing really to do with the search. Then fortune smiled. One of Chouinard's men found the cat in the rafters of a garage and managed to capture it after the old tom clawed him up a bit.

Hughes was delighted and called Chouinard. But when Chouinard mentioned that one man had been clawed a new crisis emerged. Hughes ordered that he be taken to the hospital immediately. Chouinard explained there were just a few scratches. But Hughes was adamant. The detective carefully called in with two progress reports on the man's condition. He simply lied and said he was excellent, although the man didn't even go to the hospital.

Jean Peters now realized she really couldn't keep the cat. So Hughes set out on another elaborate project, to find a good home for it. He had Romaine executives checking foster-home prospects to place the cat but couldn't settle on the credentials of the few people they found.

Eventually it was decided to send the cat to a "hostelry for cats." Chouinard was in the Romaine Street office when all this was being checked out. It was a very expensive boarding arrangement. Each cat had its own room, decorated in different colors. And one of the requirements was that the owner had to write the cat once a month while it was being boarded there.

A new employee, Harry, an Australian, was handling the affair at Romaine Street and asked incredulously if the cats read the letters. That wasn't the idea, he was told. The cat could smell the owner's letter and it made the feline feel more secure.

The girl at the cat hotel explained they also had television for the cats. The Australian was even more puzzled. "What's their favorite program?" he asked.

"Oh, I suppose Roller Derby," the girl replied.

The cat was shipped to the cat hotel and among his other duties the Australian was assigned the chore of writing the cat once a month.

CHAPTER 10

IF HOUSING AND ANIMALS WERE CONSTANT CONCERNS, transportation was no easier. One would suppose a billionaire could manage to keep himself in decent autos. But like everything else with which the Old Man became involved, it turned into a donnybrook that never ended.

Hughes had acquired a fixation on Chevrolets years before Chouinard joined him. It was the only car to buy. He insisted that Romaine keep a worn fleet of them and that black was the perfect color. He personally preferred an inconspicuous sedan and usually drove one from the fleet kept in the lot adjoining the offices.

When he had a date it was another matter. He'd order Romaine to get a Cadillac or Lincoln Continental to impress the girl of the moment—even though he insisted no one actually buy or rent one. While he saw expensive cars as a waste of money he was equally firm about their importance as implements of romance. He'd worked out his own method for acquiring these toys. Romaine would call a dealer and ask for a big sedan to try out. The dealer was always eager when he was assured that a sale to Hughes was in the offing.

Days would stretch into weeks. The dealer would start to call. Romaine would stall. The pressure would get worse as the annoyed dealer would demand the car's return or a signed sales contract. But Romaine would be fearful of asking the Old Man for the car. Finally someone would have to call him and explain the situation. As often as not he'd get a chewing out before Hughes would reluctantly surrender the auto.

Two other complications came from this system. Sometimes Hughes would call an hour before he wanted a new car. There would be a frantic scramble to find a dealer who'd deliver a new demonstrator immediately. There was no chance to cheat as the Old Man always insisted the auto be spanking new. He'd check the mileage and tires to be sure they weren't foisting off a worn relic with fifty or a hundred miles on it. As years passed and dealers, one by one, became wary after being burned in this fashion, Romaine had a more and more difficult time. A file of Cadillac and Continental dealers was maintained and notations made to rotate the dealers still vulnerable. Chouinard wandered in one morning to find a young Mormon in a high state of jubilation. He asked him why he was so happy. "They've opened a new Caddy agency out in the Valley and another Lincoln agency over near Pasadena," he said enthusiastically. He had two new victims to prey upon before they too became disenchanted.

Expensive autos weren't the only luxury items Hughes felt were foolish investments. He also refused to buy hearing aids, which he wore in private but never publicly. One clerk was assigned the task of keeping records of hearing-aid companies and writing for demonstrator models for the Old Man to test. As with the autos, Hughes would keep them until the firm was ready to threaten suit, then return them and start using a new aid on a trial basis. Meanwhile he'd use a phone amplifier for calls.

If he was penurious to the point of being a bunko artist about some matters he was extravagant to the extreme in other ways that would leave Bill Gay in a hopeless rage in business dealings. When he moved from the Beverly Hills Hotel to Bel Air he refused to give up the quarters he'd rented in the hotel and insisted no one was to use them. He kept the entire third-floor wing of the hotel itself for several years and five bungalows as well. The total cost along with catered meals and other services for Hughes and some of the staff was $3,300,000 one year, Chouinard was told.

CHAPTER

11

ONE REASON HUGHES WAS SO SUCCESSFUL IN RECRUITING young girls as starlets was the enthusiastic cooperation he usually received from their greedy mothers. These women all seemed eager to catapult their teen-age daughters to stardom by any means possible.

Terry Moore, a Morman girl, must have been fifteen when Chouinard first started following her and filing reports on her activities.

Hughes used to meet her late at night at an empty lot across from Warner Brothers' studio. She'd arrive with her mother, who would park half a block away, and the girl would walk down to the dark sedan where the Old Man awaited her. Chouinard would be parked across the street. They'd sit in the car about an hour and a half and then Terry would return to her mother's car and drive away.

This pattern went on in a haphazard manner for a time while Hughes continued to keep other girls in leased apartments and houses. Then Terry Moore married football star Glenn Davis. One afternoon after Terry had been married about a month Chouinard got a call from the Old Man at the Beverly Hills Hotel. "Jeff, I want you to come here and pick up an envelope and go to Balboa to mail it. Hurry right over."

One of the Old Man's drivers handed him the envelope in front of the bungalow. It had a handwritten address made out to Davis. The driver whispered to him, "She's in there with him and wants Davis to think she's visiting a girlfriend down at Balboa."

A week later Hughes called the detective again to pick up another envelope. He didn't relish the long drive to Balboa and back again just to mail a letter, but there it was. The letter was addressed to Davis at his home. Chouinard could feel a wedding ring inside. His instructions this time were to deliver the letter to Davis personally and then tail him.

Chouinard drove to Terry's family home in Glendale, and Davis answered the door. He handed him the envelope. He went back to his car, and ten minutes later Davis came out, appearing very agitated, and drove off. He followed him to a hospital, where Terry's mother was ill, as it turned out, and visited her.

Chouinard called in his report and guessed that another case was closed. He hadn't reckoned with the anger of Davis. A few days later Davis stalked the Old Man down at the hotel and caught him on a path behind the building. He pummeled Hughes into unconsciousness and left him bleeding in the grass. Within an hour the Old Man was on his way to San Francisco for treatment in a hospital, and Hughes' aides were swarming everywhere at the hotel to be sure the incident was covered up. It nearly was. Only one San Francisco columnist got wind of it and reported the Old Man's visit to the Bay City for medical repairs. There was nothing in the Los Angeles newspapers.

The Old Man was back in town within a few days and called Chouinard. He wanted a close tail on Davis and his every move reported. He wanted to worry Davis.

Chouinard picked up the burly athlete's car to tail it himself. Davis must have known enough about the Hughes methods to have been on the alert because within a few blocks he slammed on his brakes, jumped out of his car, and came rushing back to Chouinard.

"You're following me," he yelled. Luckily the detective only had the window open a crack and had locked the doors. Davis looked as though he might give Chouinard the same one-two he'd given Hughes.

"You're crazy," the detective replied.

"If I ever catch you in back of me again, you're in for trouble," Davis said.

"Well, maybe you'll be in trouble, too," Chouinard replied weakly.

"You don't know who I am," Davis said.

"You don't know who I am either." After this asinine exchange Davis went back to his auto and started off again. Chouinard continued to follow him even closer.

Davis stopped again. Chouinard was sure he was going to tear him apart this time, but he adopted a new approach.

"Look, I'll give you four times what you're getting if you'll tell me who you're working for."

"You don't have money enough for that," he said bravely.

Davis studied him a minute, then went back to his car. Chouinard continued to trail him for several days. Davis was fully aware of it but made no more efforts to frighten him. He stayed with Davis until the athlete took off for Texas to go to work for an oil company.

CHAPTER 12

THERE ARE SOME WHO WILL CONCLUDE THAT HUGHES trapped and enticed a young innocent as a spider catches flies. It didn't work that way.

One of the inner secrets of the organization was how easy it was for a girl to reject Hughes if she wanted to. He was shy and quick to panic if a girl had a mind of her own. While the game was to create the illusion that Howard Hughes was so all-powerful, rich, and vindictive that unless a woman gave in to his every wish her career was finished, the opposite was true. Anyone who told him to go to hell might face a brief flurry of threats but the Old Man seemed to lose all interest immediately in pursuing the matter.

Hughes brought Gina Lollobrigida, the Italian beauty, over under contract from Italy. He'd once rejected her on the basis of a photograph when she was an unknown but had decided she was worth cultivating after she became a big star. He installed her at the Town House, and security was ordered to put her under obvious surveillance. Chouinard doesn't know Hughes' motives for this as he usually wanted the men to be secretive.

Gina was a happily married woman and maybe Hughes decided the best technique was to try to frighten her into submission. If that was his plan, it worked part way. Chouinard had two men stationed at each end of the hall where she had her suite. She'd open the door a crack, peer out, and duck back in. It was obvious she was badly frightened.

After she'd been there a few days Hughes called her for dinner at the hotel. She agreed. He arrived very late as usual. By the time they got to the large hotel dining room it was ready to be closed. He quickly sent an aide over to pay the orchestra to stay and sent more money to the chef and headwaiter to continue service. It was like one of those old romantic movies when a tuxedoed hero keeps a nightclub open all night while he dances with his lady love to "our song." Yawning waiters stood about, guards came and went discreetly, the full orchestra played softly on and on while the couple dined and danced. She seemed a bit subdued by it all. But when he escorted her back to her suite at 3 A.M. he was back out within a few minutes, shouting angrily for the borrowed limousine.

The next day the heavy artillery arrived. Some of the Old Man's lawyers moved in. They told Gina she was under contract, that she'd never work in the U.S. again if she wasn't more cooperative or tried to leave the country. It didn't work. She stealthily packed her bags a few days later and departed for Rome. She never did make a picture in this country. Maybe that was because she'd seen enough of Hollywood.

Chouinard recalls other women who simply told the Old Man to get lost. Gayle Ganley, under contract to Hughes, ignored him completely. Detectives had her under surveillance for two years, but she had a boyfriend and refused even to talk to the Old Man on the phone. Chouinard is sure she never even saw him. When she was threatened by his lawyers she filed suit and collected, claiming Hughes kept her from becoming a star.

If "good girls" were a plague, sometimes "bad girls" could cause problems just as serious. One case that gave everyone fits of laughter was the raven-haired beauty who arrived from Miami. She was quickly installed in an apartment on Sunset Boulevard and routine surveillance began. As usual, no one knew who had found her and shipped her to Los Angeles.

She went sedately to bed the first evening but at seven the

next morning came sauntering out of the apartment house and up to a man in the surveillance car in front.

"Hi, honey," she said. "Would you go over to a drugstore and get me some aspirin?"

The man was in panic. They weren't accustomed to being accosted so brazenly. "I don't know what you're talking about," he stammered. "I'm waiting here for my wife."

She smiled. "Look, honey. I know who you are and how this whole Hughes thing works. Just be sweet and get me some aspirin. Huh?"

He drove away and returned in a few minutes with the aspirin. She was waiting in front and invited herself into the car. Her proposition was simplicity itself. She'd pay the surveillance man to drive her around. She had a little black book of johns in Los Angeles a girlfriend in Miami had given her. She'd call them and wouldn't turn any tricks at the apartment. But until Mr. Hughes showed up it was foolish to waste time and money!

The man reported it to Chouinard that morning. The detective didn't want to be the one to call the Old Man and tell him he had a whore on his hands, so he called Romaine instead. There was the usual panic, but someone finally got the word to Hughes. The orders came back to drop all surveillance. The girl was moved out the next day. Chouinard heard later that The Boss was outraged at what had happened.

If such immorality irritated the Old Man, he was shocked at other events. Chouinard recalls reminiscing at dinner one night in Las Vegas with Jimmy Vernon, who was the Old Man's girl finder in the casinos, and Walter Kane. They were recalling the time they'd both been called on the carpet by The Boss, who sat at a desk with a budget sheet spread out before him.

"I've just been going over what you two have been spending," he said. "How in the world can the two of you spend a million dollars in one year?"

Jimmy was always brash and carefree. "Mr. Hughes, it wasn't easy," he blithely replied. The Old Man glared at him, then began to recite the items: hotel rooms, chartered planes, dinners, autos, on and on.

Jimmy used to drink a lot. The first thing he did every morning was finish off half a bottle of Black and White Scotch. Hughes knew of this but somehow forgave him and even seemed to like his brawling, casual style.

Only Jimmy could have gotten away with one suggestion he made to the Old Man. The Boss had him under fire again for spending so much money on all the planes and other trimmings involved in finding potential starlets for the Hughes stable. "I've got one answer on how to cut costs, Mr. Hughes," he volunteered. The Boss wanted to know what it was.

"Well, I was talking to this actress over at the Flamingo the other night. I suggested I fly her over to LA for a screen test. You know what she told me? 'Tell Howard Hughes I don't want any goddamned screen test. But I'll screw him for five hundred dollars!' "

The Old Man was aghast. The actress in question went on to better things and ended up as a contessa in Italy. It was all part of the paradox that The Boss seemed to be seeking innocence and purity while those who recruited for him seemed to think he was after lusty bawds.

Chouinard doesn't know who found the Junoesque, blond "Hughes' discovery." The first word he had of her was that "some dame from Sweden" was getting her teeth fixed and he was assigned to follow her. He assumed it was another import of no consequence. Later she was to become a star in the U. S. and Europe.

Chouinard discovered she was a voluptuous Scandinavian,

what the office clique defined as a "nymphomaniac," and the source of constant anecdotes among the drivers and Romaine clerks.

As far as keeping track of her, his own duties were rather casual. She'd apparently been put on the payroll by some mysterious means, and he gathered that the Old Man hadn't met her and probably didn't even know he was supporting her.

Either she liked to shock or was truly so involved in sex that she talked of nothing else. Whatever the reason, story after story would pop up of her sex-laden conversations with Hughes' employees.

Chouinard recalls one time when he was passing a few hours at Romaine when the conversation somehow turned to the question of whether a male dog with a bulblike swelling in his penis during erection would get hung up in a girl in those South American dog-and-pony sex shows, as he would in a female dog.

One colleague giggled. "I know where to find out," he said, dialing a number.

Our blond sexologist answered, listened as he tried delicately to pose the problem. "Oh, shit yes!" she trilled and then went on in more detail than they needed to hear of techniques for a girl to get out of such a terrible situation.

By then she was a major concern to Romaine, although it seemed The Boss didn't know she existed. One driver had gone to the house to which they'd moved her from Westside Manor and found her nude at the pool, sunning herself. She'd more or less tried to rape the poor chap and he'd fled back to Romaine in panic. There was a summit meeting, and it was decided two drivers would be assigned to pick her up on all future assignments.

Then word came out of the blue that Hughes was planning to meet the blond marvel in Palm Springs the next weekend. A limousine arrived at the appointed time to pick her up. She had a huge dog in tow and set out for the desert and the rendezvous. En route she went down on the Mormon driver, who later told of the incident.

The Old Man and the dog took an immediate dislike to one another. Hughes complained that he wouldn't leave the animal in the suite, and the actress shrilled that she wanted to take the dog with her to dinner. A compromise of sorts was reached when Hughes called and ordered a rented auto. It turned out to be a convertible. He ordered it parked in front of where they were staying and the dog locked inside.

The Old Man and the svelte blonde took off for dinner at the Racquet Club, Charlie Farrell's posh haven for the movie set. It didn't last long. Her brazen talk and loud vulgarities had Hughes on edge within ten minutes. He looked around in terrible embarrassment as shocked diners at nearby tables stared at them. "Excuse me for a moment," he said. "I have to get some aspirin."

He left the dining room near the tennis courts, made it down the walk to the gate, and got into the limousine. "Take me to Los Angeles," he said.

When the dust had cleared, Hughes' aides took her back to the suite only to discover the dog had taken his own vengeance. He'd chewed up the upholstery as well as the steering wheel, then torn his way through a gap he'd ripped out in the canvas top of the rented auto.

They got her into another car and started back for Los Angeles. But she was on a rampage, cursing and shouting. As the driver reached Sunset Boulevard she spotted Walter Kane's apartment. She jumped out at a stoplight and ran to the door, pounding and screaming vulgarities. Hughes was with Walter and panicked. The Old Man called Romaine for help. Some drivers came rushing over to subdue her and hauled her away while she continued to shout wild obscenities.

The next day Chouinard was told to put her under full surveillance and Hughes went into hiding, fearful that she'd somehow break through the screen and find him. It didn't last long. She was taken off the payroll a few weeks later and faded away.

But her dog had a good time.

CHAPTER 13

IF SOME MOTHERS WERE CLUMSY OPPORTUNISTS, OTHERS were grand operators. The award of "Mother of the Year" goes to a lady who was pure pecan pie and yams.

This mother and three of her children suddenly appeared from North Carolina. As always, no one had any idea how Hughes had found them. Chouinard's first orders came when they were already installed in an apartment on Highland Avenue, in a pleasant, sedate neighborhood. There was the genteel, refined mother, a true flower of the Old South, a teenage boy and his slightly older sister and—the Hughes prize—a beautiful, fifteen-year-old blonde, with a surprising forty-inch bosom. She was given a contract, and the ritual of daily lessons began with the Hughes drivers picking her up early each morning.

Chouinard's man was staked out in an auto half a block away. After five days Chouinard got a call from the Old Man. "You've been had over there. They've spotted you," Hughes announced.

"They couldn't have. They're just saying that."

"The girl has been watching your man from the bedroom window with binoculars. She just called me."

"I don't believe it," the detective said.

"Yesterday he had a cocker spaniel in the car and was eating chocolate cake. Does that convince you?" There was no denying he'd been had all right!

"Why don't we handle it differently then," Chouinard suggested. "If you'll call them and tell them you have some people after you—Communists, other studios who want to steal the girl or something—and you want to send a guard from the studio over to take care of it, they'll understand. They haven't seen me up close."

The Old Man agreed.

The next day Chouinard arrived and knocked on the door. He'd staked a car half a block down the street with one of his men sitting in it.

The mother answered the door.

"I'm from RKO," Chouinard said. "Mr. Hughes sent me over. Has someone been bothering you?"

The mother pointed to the man in the car down the street. "He just keeps parking there, and we're concerned."

Chouinard nodded sagely. "I'll take care of that."

He strolled down to the car. "Burn some rubber," he ordered.

The man drove away and the detective sauntered back. The mother, still standing at the door, was smiling.

"Mr. Hughes wants to have a car stationed here from now on to be sure this doesn't happen again," he explained. She was delighted and flattered over the attention Mr. Hughes was giving the family.

Shortly after, the Old Man decided to upgrade the family. He ordered them moved to a large old Spanish house on Angelo Drive in Beverly Hills. It had a lovely patio, pool, and ornate, grilled windows. Chouinard had a regular twenty-four-hour shift parked in the driveway. He took one shift, a moonlighting police intelligence officer from Glendale another, and a college kid the third.

Soon the neighbors began to wonder. He found out later that a notorious Los Angeles gambler, Guy McAfee, had a house just down the street and—although he was dead—his daughter still lived there. Neighbors were skittish and thought Chouinard was part of a gangster mob.

Chouinard noticed a car staked out down the street. He got the license number, checked it through, and called the number. A woman answered the phone.

"This is the Retail Credit Company," he said. "I just want to update a few records."

She answered a few routine questions about her address and then he asked if her husband still had the same job. "Oh, yes," she said. "He's been a reporter for the *Examiner* for twenty years."

Chouinard suspected that one of the neighbors had called the paper. A few days later it became apparent that the reporter must have gone to Chief Anderson at the Beverly Hills Police Department to find out what was going on. Anderson had been a man Chouinard had always avoided. Ordinarily the detective would have asked for his cooperation on Hughes' operations in Beverly Hills considering they had so many leased houses and apartments in the city. But Anderson was such a publicity hound Chouinard was afraid he'd expose their operations at some point just to get newspaper space.

Now two plainclothesmen in a Beverly Hills police car pulled up in front of the house, got out, and walked over to Chouinard sitting in the auto in the driveway. They identified themselves. "What are you doing here?"

"I'm on private property. I'm a bodyguard for these people."

They persisted, wanting to know whom he worked for, why

he'd been hired. He wasn't going to show his identification as a private detective as he knew it would simply escalate their interest.

"Have you got a Beverly Hills license to be a bodyguard?" one asked.

"No," he answered.

"Okay. Then we're going to take you in."

He was trapped. "All right," he replied. "Just let me go in and tell the lady of the house that I have to go."

He went into the house and promptly locked the door, telling the brother to lock the back door.

"Don't worry," he told the distraught mother. "I'll handle this."

He went to the phone and called The Boss, who was in Las Vegas. When he explained the problem the Old Man began to chuckle. It appealed to his sense of cops-and-robbers intrigue.

"You mean you're on the inside and they're on the outside and there's no way they can get in?"

He held the phone toward the door where the two furious cops were pounding. "It's thick as hell and we've got those iron grills on the windows," he replied.

"Great! Don't let them in. I'll have them off your ass in no time."

He went confidently back to the door and opened the large peephole.

"Get out here. You're going to jail for resisting arrest," one yelled, continuing to hammer at the oak door.

Chouinard thought he'd have some fun while he waited. "Are you guys with the police department or working for the *Examiner*?" he asked. "You should be working for the taxpayers, not for some damned newspaper."

"Get out here right now," the cop shouted.

"I'm going to write a letter to the Beverly Hills *Citizen* telling them how you work for a downtown newspaper at taxpayers' expense," he said. "In a little while someone is going to come and get you and tell you to get back to work."

Sure enough, within a half hour a Beverly Hills patrol car pulled up and the two plainclothesmen went over, chatted with the uniformed cop and, giving baleful stares at the house, got into their car and drove away. The Old Man had indeed gotten them off his neck with one fast call.

The mother was constantly asking Chouinard about Mr. Hughes and gushing over what a lonesome, sweet, and kindly gentleman he must be. Hughes avoided her at all costs and regularly refused her endless invitations to a "real home-cooked meal." He did issue instructions to the mother that she followed assiduously. The girl must sleep in her bra every night, and she was never, never to turn her head more than fifteen degrees or it might put lines in her neck. The drivers were cautioned as usual never to cross railroad tracks and to slow down to two miles an hour at bumps to avoid injuring the girl's breast tissue.

The solicitous mother began to question more and more the lack of progress in her daughter's career. Hughes soothed her on the phone, explaining that her daughter was marked for stardom. "She's the most beautiful girl since Billie Dove," he told the mother, "and will be one of the biggest movie stars of all time."

Yet the months passed. Then the mother started pressing Hughes to take her daughter and her on a trip to the desert, which she said she'd never seen. The end came with the speed of light. Hughes took the mother and daughter to Palm Springs one weekend. The story became office gossip soon after.

The mother set The Boss up with the girl in a brazen way and then broke in, her refined Southern-matron image wiped away.

"You filthy, dirty, old bastard," she screamed. "You've ruined my daughter and she's only sixteen! I'm going to sue you and spread this story around the world. You're going to prison this time."

It was settled out of court. A prominent attorney, a friend of Noah Dietrich, handled the matter. It cost $250,000. Aides calculated that the whole affair, with the trimmings, must have come closer to a half million. Hughes never mentioned the girl again.

CHAPTER 14

WHY, AIDES OFTEN PONDERED, DID THE OLD MAN ALWAYS have such a rube's fascination with actresses? Why he found alluring a small-town girl or Brooklyn chorine who'd taken some drama lessons, learned how to handle a cocktail fork, and schooled herself to use a broad British "a" to pose as a lady always amazed them. By the time Chouinard knew Hughes he'd long ago discarded the famed movie stars he'd been seen with, but the Old Man continued friendly relations with many of them. The smell of greasepaint would never completely leave.

One of the detective's first assignments for The Boss, when Chouinard was still working for the security agent the Old Man had asked him to replace, grew out of Hughes' friendship with Franchot Tone. Chouinard was still raw and new to the whole world of being a sleuth when he was ordered to start spying on party girl and would-be actress Barbara Payton. The detective was in a bar when Hughes called him with instructions.

"Franchot Tone is a friend of mine," he explained. "I want you to get over to the house where Barbara Payton lives and report to me what's going on." Chouinard had, of course, read the news stories. A would-be actor and boxer, Tom Neal, had beaten Tone up in a nightclub quarrel over the sexy blonde. Tone was in the hospital, and Neal had moved in with Payton. Hughes went on to explain that he'd told Tone weeks before to get rid of her, that she was "nothing but a whore."

"He told me, 'Maybe so, but she's the best piece of ass I've ever had,' " Hughes quoted Tone as replying. "I want to show him she's a bad woman. I want you to get up there and prove it for me so I can present Franchot with some facts," The Boss directed, "but don't let anyone know you're working for me."

Chouinard didn't know where to start but began by parking his car right behind her auto on a steep incline in front of her house. He went to her door and knocked. She answered, wearing a pair of shorts and a halter. She was voluptuous.

"I'm sorry, but my battery is dead. Can you move your car so I can get out?" he asked.

"Sure," she readily agreed and came out to move the car. He went down the hill and waved to her—wondering what he'd accomplished by that move.

He returned an hour later with a woman detective and parked nearby, puzzling what to do next. It didn't take long to find out. Two plainclothes policemen pulled up in a black sedan beside them.

"What are you doing here?" one thin, asthmatic-appearing clod asked. Obviously they had the house under surveillance due to the furor in the press.

"Nothing," said Chouinard. "I'm just a private citizen sitting here."

Within ten minutes the detective and his partner were in an interrogation room at the Hollywood police station. The police emptied Chouinard's wallet and found nothing important.

There was nothing to show he was a private detective. They questioned him, found out he was married, looked up his home phone number.

"So you're out with a girl," one said. "How'd you like it if we called your wife?"

"You wouldn't do anything like that," he said.

"No?" The detective dialed all but the last number of his home phone and paused. "Will you tell us what you were doing there?"

Chouinard shook his head. "That's too damned dirty and low for anyone to do," he complained. "I was just sitting there."

Apparently the reply somehow convinced the officer that he was just an errant husband playing around. He hung up. They let Chouinard and the woman detective go, but warned them to stay away from the area.

The next night Chouinard was back, parked on the street. The detectives pulled up. "Are you nuts?" one demanded. "We told you to stay away. There are things going on around here."

This time Chouinard flashed his identification, showing he was a private detective.

"You dumb son of a bitch. Why didn't you tell us that yesterday?"

"I wasn't working yesterday. Today I am."

They called his boss, whom they both knew, and verified that he was on a job. "What kind of a nut have you got working for you anyway?" they asked him.

"He's just green," his boss explained. When he got back to the office the boss told him he didn't have to hold out and be a martyr in such a situation.

He didn't ever establish that Barbara Payton was really a whore until years later when she died, a fat, bloated junkie working in a brothel in the Negro district of Los Angeles.

CHAPTER
15

IN CHOUINARD'S EARLY YEARS WITH HUGHES, THE BILLIONAIRE developed a fondness for Jean Simmons, the actress, who was married to Stewart Granger at the time. Hughes gave her parts in one or two movies, and it was obvious he was fascinated with her. Granger, who fancied himself an astute businessman, gave Hughes endless woe acting as her manager, demanding more and more money and generally being unpleasant. Aides don't know how it came about, but eventually Hughes agreed to buy Granger's house. There was bickering and bitterness, and it appeared that the matter was going to court.

The Old Man called Chouinard one day and told him to meet him at the parking lot of the East Gate to Bel Air. Hughes was waiting in a battered Romaine car-pool Chevrolet under a sycamore tree. He handed Chouinard some legal papers. "Deliver these to Stewart Granger," he said, giving him an address on Bel Air Road. "I'll wait here. I know he's home right now."

It appeared odd to be personally handling something it seemed a lawyer should be doing, but the detective made the delivery and returned.

"Did you get them to him?" Hughes asked. Chouinard said he had. Hughes was happy, thanked him, and drove off.

Soon after, the Old Man ordered full surveillance on Granger and Jean Simmons. It was routine until the day they drove to the airport and kissed good-bye as Granger prepared to leave. As Chouinard knew he could now be careless, he moved close to them. Granger stared directly at him. At least that's over, he thought. He called Hughes to tell him of Granger's departure.

"All right," the Old Man said in the emphatic way that the detective had learned meant there was more to come. "Now I want you to go to Europe tomorrow and tail him there. I want you to stick right with him." Chouinard was startled. He told Hughes of how Granger had stared at him at the airport and reminded Hughes that he'd probably seen him deliver the legal papers. "Actors never notice anyone else," Hughes replied. "Don't worry about it. Grow a moustache."

"But it's three thirty in the afternoon and I don't even have a passport. There's no way I can get one."

Hughes was not to be put aside. "Get over and apply for one right now. Then call me," he ordered. "I'll take care of the rest."

Chouinard drove to the passport office. A small Japanese clerk was polite but told him it took thirty days. He called Hughes back with the news.

"No, no," The Boss replied. "It doesn't take thirty days. Did you apply?"

He said he had.

"Fine. Now you get on the plane tomorrow. Someone will meet you in New York and have your passport." The shock of such a trip, which was a big thing in those days, had worn off, and he decided to go for broke. It could be fun.

"Mr. Hughes," he asked. "Could I take my wife?" There was a silence. "Traveling alone, I may be easy to spot as a detective. But with my wife we'll just look like a tourist couple," he continued weakly.

"Good idea," Hughes replied suddenly. "Call her and have her apply for a passport, too. I'll take care of it."

They were met the next evening by a TWA man in New York who handed them their passports. How Hughes had managed it in twenty-four hours Chouinard doesn't know. He also had arranged for the Chouinards to get a TWA red-carpet letter, such as VIP's are given, and they were to be met by limousines and chauffeurs everywhere they went. They couldn't even spend a dime for a phone call.

Hughes called him again that night before they departed. "I want a full report on everything he does," he explained. "Who he sees, who he eats with, if he takes out a girl, who she is, what she does . . ."

Belatedly, the purpose of his task dawned on Chouinard. He was to catch Granger playing hanky-panky games away from home so Hughes could snitch to Jean Simmons! The Old Man then gave him Granger's hotel in Paris and wished him good luck.

When they arrived, Granger had already departed for Rome. It was the middle of the day and they'd never been in Paris before. Damned if Chouinard would miss it! He booked tickets to Rome for the next day and they made a hurried sightseeing tour of the city.

The next afternoon they were in Rome. But Granger had already departed for Palermo. Again, they paused for the rest of the day to have a look at Rome and took off the next morning for Palermo. The detective knew he must be getting close to Granger by now and was wary about making inquiries. But he soon found out that Granger had left for a converted monastery that was now a fashionable hotel at Taormina on the eastern side of Sicily. By now Chouinard was sure Granger had some assignation arranged and he'd be able to give the Old Man the report he wanted. They flew to Catania only to find they had fifty miles north still to go by taxi to reach the hotel. Worse still, no cab driver would take them. A notorious bandit, Giuliano, was on the loose, ambushing tourists, and no cabbie wanted to be on a country road.

Then he found one driver who could be bribed. He spoke only a fragmented English and Chouinard knew no Italian. The driver kept trying to teach him a phrase that Chouinard was to say in Italian when they reached an army checkpoint, meanwhile warning him not to say another Italian sentence. All along the way the driver kept coaching him. The detective assumed it had something to do with saying he was with the State Department or on official business.

If the driver hadn't told him what not to say he would have been all right. But he blurted it out to the officers at the post in his excitement. He doesn't know what it was all about, but they grabbed the driver and hauled him into a little shack. A half hour later he came out glaring angrily at Chouinard and swearing in Italian. He drove them on to the hotel but refused to speak to them. Even when Chouinard tipped him heavily he didn't thank him and before he drove off gave him one of those Italian hand-in-the-crook-of-the-arm insults. Chouinard figures he must have done something awfully wrong.

At least they had caught up with Granger, he thought. The next morning he found a bellboy and subtly inquired. "Mr. Granger? He left yesterday," the youth replied. Chouinard found out from the desk that he'd gone on to Tunis in North Africa. Wearily they packed again, retraced their route to Palermo, and flew on to Tunis.

At last they found him at a hotel, with the cast and crew of an MGM movie that Richard Brooks was directing. They registered at the hotel and sat back to observe. By the second day Chouinard had managed to get himself invited out to the desert where the filming was going on. Renting a car, they set out, soon making a wrong turn in the barren sands. At an Arab village they tried to make inquiries in French. Chouinard hadn't realized how strong the anti-French sentiment was and soon had a mob of mean-faced Arabs milling around the auto. Just when he was becoming panicked he saw a half dozen black French Legionnaires—he believes they're called Senegalese—moving toward them. They saved the bacon.

That was his last venture into the desert. He took to loafing around the hotel bar, chatting with the cast when they came in from a day of shooting. The Chouinards identified themselves as a rich couple from California on their second honeymoon.

They struck up an acquaintance with Granger and took to drinking with him each evening. The detective would ask Granger what he did, where he went each day, and get a handy report from the horse's mouth. Disappointingly, he could file no report that Granger was unfaithful to Jean Simmons. Each night Chouinard would sit in a pay phone booth, unscrewing the tiny light bulb to darken it, and watch Granger's door down the corridor, checking him in each night and up each morning with nothing to report.

The days passed. When they sat at the table having drinks each evening only one man, Richard Brooks, seemed suspicious of him. Brooks would stare at him continually, saying nothing, but Chouinard had the uneasy feeling he knew more about him than he'd say. Ironically, Brooks was to marry Jean Simmons years later.

Hughes had warned the detective to be sure to call him the day shooting ended and Granger started back. When that day came he made the call, then they took a plane to Paris. It was a good thing Chouinard hadn't been trying to do his sleuthing on a TWA plane, for on the way back the pilot made a big thing of coming out to greet them and saying, "You're a friend of Mr. Hughes, I understand."

Aboard the flight was Ralph Damon, who was president of TWA. The pilot took him over to meet Damon. He was a courtly and distinguished older man, who'd once been president of Curtiss-Wright and was from his home state. They had a pleasant chat about Maine.

After a time the executive paused. "Tell me, are you a friend of Mr. Hughes'?" he inquired.

"Oh, yes," Chouinard said casually.

"You know a strange thing? I've been running his airline

for many years and I've never met him in person. What sort of a fellow is he?"

He didn't have the heart—a brash, young man of twenty-eight—to tell this important executive that he saw more of Mr. Hughes than he wished.

"Well, I've never met him in person either," he lied.

Damon seemed relieved and pleased.

When they arrived in New York he had one more brief moment of glory when the TWA escort arrived again with the limousine for the final red-carpet treatment.

Chouinard asked the chauffeur to drive to Elizabeth, New Jersey, where his uncle Pete worked as a short-order cook. He and his wife pulled up in the limousine and his uncle came out of the kitchen, almost weeping at his success. Chouinard told him only that he was associated with Howard Hughes.

When Chouinard got home and called Hughes, the Old Man said he wasn't interested in seeing the elaborate report the detective had put together. "All I want to know is if that guy slept with any women," he said, which was exceedingly blunt for Hughes.

"No," he replied.

"That shitass!" Hughes said irritably and hung up.

His interest in Jean Simmons didn't end after the African trip. At one point Jean told Walter Kane that she and Granger weren't getting along at all. "But he's so money-minded and I owe him twenty thousand dollars," she complained. "If I could throw it in his face, I'd walk out on him."

Walter called the Old Man immediately. "Hell, yes, give it to her. But be sure to get a receipt."

Walter was shocked. "Howard, you can't do that. Not in a situation like this."

The Old Man wouldn't budge, romantic interest or not. "Walter, you have to understand. It's bad business to give money away without a receipt. Then it's not deductible. It's just not the way to do things."

The next time Jean Simmons stopped by Walter's apartment he hesitantly approached the matter. "You know that money you owe Stewart. Howard wants to pay him off. He'll give you the money but he wants you to sign a receipt."

"Forget it," she snapped, and left. It ended the potential romance.

CHAPTER 16

THE INCIDENT WAS TYPICAL OF HUGHES' PECULIAR SENSE of business. He refused to go to any meeting or to an office. He made his own decisions alone and dictated them over the phone to his assistants. He constantly lost memos of great importance, sticking them in a rear pants pockets until they became crumpled and then throwing them away.

But even with all the failures he showed occasional flashes of business brilliance that stunned all around him. Years later, just before he started buying up Las Vegas property, when he was seemingly close to a vegetable in the Bel Air room, he issued orders to start buying Lockheed executive jets. They were lavish and expensive, several million dollars each, and he ordered five of them. The executives at Romaine were frantic with worry. Everyone knew that all the top aircraft firms were coming out with executive jets and that the Lockheed model was too costly. But the Old Man would listen to no one. The jets were stored and everyone sat back ready to watch them decline in value month by month. The opposite happened as businessmen started trying to get the same model and waiting lists grew. Hughes sold his off one by one and made a huge killing.

When he faced the revolt of executives at RKO in 1954 he pulled another ploy that left everyone stunned. A syndicate from Chicago came to Hughes with a $1½ million down payment. The backers were suspected of gangster connections, and Hughes knew the deal would never go through. But he took the money, and not long after, a story was planted in the *Wall Street Journal* telling of the pending sale of RKO. Pressure mounted from all directions and in the end Hughes kept most of the down payment and RKO was sold to General Tire and Rubber Company.

The Old Man handled the whole maneuver so adroitly that the Chicago syndicate never realized what had happened. The next Christmas they even sent him a gold watch in appreciation of what he'd tried to do for them. He was so surprised at the gift that he shook his head and began to chuckle. "Goddamn! They spent their dough on me after what I did to them!"

Some of his financial dealings weren't as earth-shaking. He was constantly calling someone to bring pocket money to bail him out of a situation. He was always embarrassed at such moments. Typical was the evening he'd taken Mitzi Gaynor to a restaurant, Larry Potter's on Ventura Boulevard, and—as usual—was trying to appear incognito. When the time came to pay the check he found he had no money. Rather than tell the management who he was and sign the check, he excused himself and went to the men's room phone and called Romaine.

He told Kay Glenn where he was and asked him to bring some money. "When you come in just walk past the table and don't act like you know me. Go to the men's room, and I'll follow you. I don't want the girl to know I'm broke."

Glenn did as directed and handed Hughes a fresh hundred-dollar bill. "Thanks," sighed Hughes. "You got me out of a terrible mess."

Kay Glenn could keep his cool under any circumstance. The Old Man trusted him completely. He was often assigned to squire new Hughes major finds around to dinner and keep them amused. This could be a tedious chore. Chouinard recalls when the Old Man had discovered a cute blond stripper. Kay was told to entertain her and see that she was happy. Unfortunately, what made her happy was seeing other strippers perform. Night after night Kay had to watch gyrating hips and bumps and grinds.

One of Chouinard and Glenn's more exciting assignments came one day in Las Vegas when Kay had been told to deliver a $21 million personal check from Hughes to a TWA pilot for delivery to New York. It was the mission of the day, and they plotted it carefully while Chouinard had drinks in various casinos and Kay, a Mormon, watched.

They did very well until they got to the airport and discovered they'd left the check in a drawer back at the Flamingo Hotel. Lesser men would have become hysterical, knowing that one of the biggest personal checks in all history had been misplaced and could be stolen by any chambermaid.

Not Glenn. "I'm Howard Hughes' personal secretary," he advised the ticket man. "I want you to hold up the plane while I go back to the hotel and get something."

The clerk stared at Glenn. "And I'm Winston Churchill's bastard son," he replied. "It's illegal to hold up airplanes, even if the pilot would stay here. How do I know you're Hughes' secretary?"

Glenn shrugged. "Look, I'm going back right now. If the plane isn't still here when I return you'll find out who I am and be looking for a new job."

It worked. They rushed back, and when they returned the

plane was still there. The pilot departed, carrying that huge personal check in his pocket and unaware of it.

CHAPTER 17

ONE MORNING THE OLD MAN CALLED AND THERE WAS AN unusual, almost apologetic, note in his voice. Chouinard didn't understand it as he was usually brisk and all business.

"Jeff, would you mind doing me a favor?"

"Whatever I can, Mr. Hughes."

"Liz Taylor is leaving today from Lockheed. She'll be getting on an old Lockheed Ten, a twin-engine job. I want you to get out there and see who she says good-bye to and if you can get their names. If not, get a good description of every one of them for me."

Chouinard went out and found the bon voyage party, checked the license numbers of those who attended, and when they went to the parking lot after the plane took off was able to call in the car owners' names to The Boss by early afternoon. Hughes thanked him and that was all.

When Liz Taylor returned she had divorced Nicky Hilton. A day or so later Hughes called him again. "Liz Taylor is back in town and I want you to put a surveillance on her. I'd appreciate it if you'd handle it yourself. She's very young and irresponsible and I'm doing this for her parents while they're in Florida. I told them I'd have someone keep an eye on her so she won't get into trouble."

Chouinard staked out in front of the apartment house just off Wilshire where both Taylor and Janet Leigh lived. All was calm for a few days as his men worked a twenty-four-hour shift. Then his brother-in-law Don Blackey, on duty at the time, called one night to say Liz appeared to be getting ready to go out. Chouinard hurried over, and when she came out to her car she was dressed for some formal affair.

He trailed her to Santa Monica, where she picked up a boy who, he discovered later, was a would-be actor from Europe. They took off to the Biltmore in downtown Los Angeles to attend a Directors' Guild dinner. He waited it out, and when they emerged in front of the hotel to get their car from the attendant they were both badly loaded. He stood right next to them, wondering what to do. They could hardly stand up and Liz began to lean on Chouinard, a complete stranger to her, while the attendant brought the car to the front.

By then it was two in the morning, and the detective began following them all the way to Santa Monica. They were weaving and zigzagging across the center line. He wondered whether to try to stop them and take the keys. If there was an accident, he knew the Old Man would blame him. He was still debating when they pulled up at last to the actor's apartment house.

Hughes received the news with a note of concern, complaining about people who allowed actresses to get drunk at official functions. "I'm going to have to get someone to escort her who I can trust," he said.

Not long after, he called and told Chouinard that he'd arranged for an old friend, Pat di Cicco, to take her out to dinner and keep her busy. "I want you to keep tabs on them and call me every forty-five minutes," Hughes ordered.

Chouinard followed them as they had drinks at one restaurant, drove to another for dinner, and settled in at a table.

He'd called in twice by then, glancing at his watch to phone at the approximate interval. His third call, Hughes spoke up immediately, before he could give any report.

"Jeff, I told you to call me every forty-five minutes," he said. "The first call was forty-four minutes and the second call forty-six and a half minutes. This one is nearly forty-seven minutes!"

Chouinard apologized. "Do you have a watch?" Hughes demanded.

He said he had.

"All right. Let's synchronize our watches so this won't happen again."

Before the night was over he was to find new wonders in the ways of Howard Hughes. The couple returned to her apartment and went in. The detective methodically reported at each forty-five-minute interval exactly. Time wore on.

Hughes sounded more and more concerned with each call.

"I'll tell you what you do," he said at last. "There's an alley behind that apartment house. Her bedroom faces the alley. There are two telephone poles about eight feet away. If you climb one of those poles you can get a good look. Take some binoculars."

Chouinard was fascinated. How did Hughes know the detailed layout behind the Taylor apartment? He went to the alley and found things as Hughes had said. But he wouldn't shimmy the pole. He told Hughes the curtains were pulled and he wouldn't have seen anything anyway.

He continued to call Hughes until around eight that morning. "Di Cicco is still up there," he had to report.

Hughes groaned. "Well, I'll be a son of a bitch! That's what you get when you ask a friend to do you a favor. That's what the bastard does to me! What am I going to tell her parents?"

Sometimes Chouinard went astray on his assignments—in

all truth—more and more often as the years passed. When The Boss called him with instructions to follow Ava Gardner down to Tijuana, where she was going to see a bullfight, he looked upon the task as a holiday and a lark. Ava was indeed an old girlfriend, but he knew Hughes hadn't seen her in years. How from the Old Man's convoluted sources of information he'd gotten word of her pending trip, Chouinard had no way of knowing. By that time the detective was too jaded to even question where Hughes' sources might be.

The mission was simple. All he had to do was tail her and see that she didn't have any trouble. "Don't get too close but don't get too far away from her," Hughes cautioned.

She was with a group and he managed to end up in a seat just behind her at the bullring. He was sitting next to an attractive, blond European girl who claimed she was an American citizen. They started talking and he offered her his bottle of tequila. Soon she was telling him that her boyfriend was a Mexican and she really hated him because he was keeping her in Mexico against her will. With the hot sun and booze Chouinard became increasingly indignant at her unhappy plight. By the time the bullfight was over and he watched Ava and her friends depart with the mayor of Tijuana for dinner he'd decided she was safe. He turned his attention to the lovely girl next to him.

As they made their way through the departing crowd she explained that her boyfriend, René, was a leading dope peddler and that his best buddy was a narcotics officer. By the time they arrived at the café where she was to meet them she had cautioned the detective to be careful or he'd be in serious trouble. Chouinard was Sir Lancelot. "I've got a rented car down the street. I'll get you to it and we'll make it across the border," he told her.

Dinner was a tense affair between the narcotics officer, René, the girl, and Chouinard. When she excused herself it was obvious Chouinard wasn't the first gringo to whom she'd told her woes. "Jeff, you're a nice guy, but if you've got any ideas of taking my girl across the border, forget it," René warned him with a smile.

By then Chouinard was drunk. When the girl returned he went to the phone and called the police. They arrived, listened politely to his story, had a drink with the narcotics cop, and started to depart.

They all went outside. Chouinard saw some U. S. sailors approaching. If he started a fracas, he drunkenly reasoned, they'd help him then. They'd all go to jail, and he could get the American Consul to help. He turned to the grinning cops. "Listen Buster! If you want trouble, I can give it to you," he threatened. Then he took a closer look at the U. S. sailors he'd hoped would leap to his aid. They all looked about thirteen.

Chouinard did soon end up at the jail, for questioning. He'd get up and they'd shove him back into a chair. He'd get up again and they'd repeat the performance. At five in the morning his butt was very sore.

"Okay, if you act good, you can go home now," a fat cop said.

"I don't want to go home," he snarled. "I want a police escort and I want to take that girl with me across the border."

"That girl doesn't want to go across the border."

"I'll have to hear that from her," he said.

They brought the girl in from the other room. "You dirty son of a bitch," she cried. "Look at the trouble you've got me in. I don't want to leave Mexico."

Chouinard asked the police to drive him to his rented car. He got in, locked the doors, and started down a dirt road for the border gate. A blue Cadillac sedan pulled up beside him and tried to force him off the road, bashing in one side of the rented car. He made it back to the U. S. singing "God Bless America."

Years later he was trying to get a drink before closing time in a sleazy bar on Santa Monica Boulevard in Los Angeles. The girl was working there as a cocktail waitress.

"It can't be you, I thought you'd be in jail somewhere by now," he said.

She glared at him. "You sure got me into a lot of trouble," she replied bitterly. "What will it be, tequila?"

Ava Gardner made it home somehow, Chouinard presumes.

CHAPTER 18

IF ACTRESSES FASCINATED HUGHES, SO DID THE SILVER screen.

When the jungle drums at Romaine sent word that the Old Man was about to go on a movie bender all were delighted. They knew it would mean at least a weekend of freedom from the nerve-jarring phone calls, sometimes as much as a week.

Chouinard would usually get a call from a crony at Romaine. "The Professor is getting his list up to date," the informant would whisper. This was the retired professor whose mission it was to compile the list of all movies he thought Hughes might want to see. He chronicled not only the title but the subject matter and a brief story line, the producer, director, actors, critical comments. The list would be sent on to the Old Man to make selections.

A heated analysis would begin. Hughes would reject one movie because the director was "a goddamned fool" and another because one of the reviews said a chase sequence was too trite. Out of this long process a final list of those pictures which met the Old Man's odd standards would be forged. It would include several cornball Westerns, foreign films filled with subtle nuances, outdated melodramas. If nothing else, his tastes were catholic.

The Professor would now start assembling the pictures at the Sam Goldwyn Studio, not far from Romaine Street, for the marathon viewing orgy that was about to begin. This would lead to new complications. Hughes could get domestic films free on a reciprocal agreement because he was technically head of a production company. But many of the foreign films cost three hundred dollars each. The Professor would be frantic as the deadline approached, trying to coax those foreign films out of distributors for nothing. If he had to pay, Hughes would often cut the picture from his selected list in a fury and complain to the Professor that he seemed to be losing his knack and could be replaced.

The next conflict would come with the projectionist at Goldwyn Studios. Romaine would start negotiating for free use of a projection room and, when that failed, try to whittle the price down. The Old Man would call constantly for progress reports and then go into orbit again when the news would come that the projectionist wanted double-time under the usual union rules. Finally he'd reluctantly agree to pay. Later he found one man who could run a projector and he moved to a cheaper projection room on Sunset Boulevard.

This led to one of his wilder capers. Jean Peters was constantly pleading with Hughes to do something about his painful piles. He'd promise again and again but procrastinate, complaining of nonexistent business involvements and pending mergers. Finally she pinned him to the wall. He agreed to go to a hospital in Boston and be treated, with one understanding. She wasn't to discuss his case with the doctors or call him while he was undergoing treatment. She was so pleased that she immediately agreed. He took off for the airport a few days later. Or so he told her.

He went, instead, to the projection room on Sunset Boulevard, where he'd laid in a huge supply of candy bars, milk, and endless cans of film. The great escapade began. He sat for weeks in that projection room. He'd sleep fitfully while his clothes got filthy and his body odor stronger and stronger. Each day he'd call Jean with a progress report, say how nice the nurses were, and complain about the New England weather. She really felt she'd accomplished something. At last he emerged from hibernation and went home—his piles worse from sitting all those weeks. She never knew.

Such lonely vigils before the screen weren't typical, however. He preferred to have companions when he settled in for an eighteen-hour stint of movie viewing. As usual he'd plot little schemes to trap people into joining him. Typically, he once cornered the Governor of Florida. The rumor was out that Hughes was planning to build an aircraft plant in West Palm Beach. It would mean a massive payroll naturally, and the Governor arrived to try to clinch the deal and be able to take credit. Hughes delegated Kay Glenn to entertain him and refused to see him for a few days. Then he agreed to meet him at the projection room.

It was futile and frustrating for the Governor. Hughes would allow no one to talk during a picture. The only break would come when the movie was stopped halfway through and a driver stood up to announce that it was time to go to the toilet. As Hughes despised anyone getting up during a picture, the urinal run was a firm routine. And a simple admission that one didn't need to go was no way out. Guests such as the Governor had to get up and at least *try*. After several nights of this ritual and no chance to even mention aircraft factories the Governor left in despair.

CHAPTER 19

HUGHES FELT HE WAS ENTITLED TO HIS OWN ESCAPES. BUT he didn't approve of holidays for others. Chouinard remembers the time he decided to sneak away without telling Hughes. He'd never taken his boy camping, so he made arrangements to go on a short back-packing trip to the Sierras. He told others where he was going and that it would only be for two or three days. The first morning Chouinard was awakened by the side of a beautiful lake by the sound of a plane. He crawled out of his sleeping bag and got up to see a twin-engine Beechcraft circling the lake slowly. He ran under a pine tree to hide. "The son of a bitch is after me and he's going to spot me and drop a package with a message in it to report immediately," he concluded.

But then he saw the plane fly low and drop fingerlings into the lake. It was a Fish and Game Department aircraft. He sighed and congratulated himself that Hughes hadn't tracked him down after all.

Everyone was acutely aware of the Hughes panic if someone wasn't available when he phoned. Once one executive, an attorney, had quietly sneaked away. He mentioned going to Big Sur. Hughes found out. Red alert! The California Highway Patrol was contacted and persuaded to put out an all-points bulletin on Highway 101. They found the unfortunate near San Simeon and told him he was to call Hughes immediately. It was life or death. The Old Man insisted the lawyer return right away as something shattering had happened. When he arrived in Los Angeles Hughes had invented a petty chore for him to do.

Some years later when Hughes was ill in the Bel Air mansion his doctor had an opportunity to go to Tahiti on a Pan Am inaugural flight. He'd been attending the Old Man for years and was desperate for some kind of vacation.

Hughes was nearly hysterical at the suggestion. "Jesus, you must be crazy!" he told the pleading doctor. "I'd never risk going on that goddamned airline. You know that I know all about planes. I just wouldn't risk it." He went on inventing stories of Pan Am's ineptness. "I'll tell you what," he concluded. "As soon as I'm a little better I'll personally charter a plane and fly you to Tahiti." The doctor stayed home.

Another of Hughes' pet peeves was being told why one of his quaint projects couldn't be done. He was always demanding the impossible and wanting it done immediately.

Chouinard recalls the summer day in 1951 when he'd been fishing on his boat off San Pedro.

There was a message for him at the dock from Romaine. The staff member read the order: He was to go immediately to Culver City, where there was a pilot and an A-20—an army-surplus light bomber—waiting to fly him to Las Vegas for an assignment.

"Hell, I'm reeking with the smell of bait and have an odor like a canning factory," Chouinard said. "I'll have to go home and change clothes first."

"No, no! There isn't time. The pilot has been waiting for two hours. The Boss has called three times already. He said to tell you to get another man to help you out."

He had to go. He called a highway patrolman in Santa Monica who worked at the Malibu station and sometimes moonlighted, who Chouinard knew was then on vacation. The patrolman was delighted to pick up some extra money and have a trip to Vegas at the same time. He agreed to meet Chouinard at the airport at Culver City.

The detective couldn't stand his own smell as he drove

through the humid, smoggy heat to the airport. His companion's nose twitched as they boarded, and the pilot grunted in disgust. When they landed in Vegas the temperature was 115 degrees. There was a car waiting.

"Take me to a men's store," Chouinard said. In the shop he picked out all new clothes while the disdainful clerk carried the old fishing clothes to the trash.

The "terrible crisis" concerned the usual. Hughes had spotted a beautiful girl at the Desert Inn. He'd given a bellhop ten dollars to follow her car and get the license number, but the bellhop hadn't been able to get it. Chouinard's orders were to find the girl again. Hughes gave him a complicated, detailed description of her size, hair, eyes, what she had been wearing. He was to report hourly. Finding a particular girl in Las Vegas with its swarms of tourists going in and out of dozens of hotels, casinos, and restaurants is impossible. He relaxed, knowing it would be a fluke of pure luck if he could spot her.

He and his partner Steve, the highway patrolman, started by interviewing desk clerks, waitresses, people running the gambling tables. Several days passed without a clue.

One afternoon Steve and Chouinard stopped at a crap table and were doing well when Chouinard looked up at his partner and found him frozen in position, dice in hand, a look of shock on his face.

Chouinard glanced around. The Old Man was standing next to him!

It was Hughes' tendency in such a situation to use the style of the old movie cliché when two undercover agents exchange information in a crowd. Looking straight ahead, Hughes whispered in his ear, a conspicuous approach that draws more attention than simply looking at one another and talking.

"Are you having any luck?" he asked conspiratorially.

"Not yet."

"Where's your partner?"

He glanced at Steve, who was still standing frozen right next to him.

"He's working the other side of the street."

Hughes, of course, didn't know Steve. "Keep it up. Keep it up," he whispered and faded away. Steve put down the dice and said he was through.

The nice part of hunting for a girl in such a situation is that one might find her anywhere. This meant they could spend money going to shows, having expensive dinners, wandering through casinos, and gambling at the tables.

They took full advantage of it at a leisurely pace. That night they decided to take in the Spike Jones show at the Flamingo. They'd ordered drinks and settled down when a beautiful redhead was introduced, doing a trampoline act. She then did a skit with another girl.

"Steve, let's do the old game plan," Chouinard suggested. It was a corny old Las Vegas gag of accosting two girls and asking them to have a drink. If they agreed, Chouinard would excuse himself to go to the men's room and Steve would explain to the girl Chouinard was with that Chouinard was a very important man. "You know who he is, don't you?" he'd begin confidentially. "His family owns the biggest lumber company in the Northwest. He's loaded." Then, when Steve excused himself, Chouinard was to tell some similar bit of hokum about Steve. It was a fine idea, but the gambit required that the girls agree to have a drink. They sent a message backstage with a waiter and waited. Nothing happened.

The next day Steve had to return to Los Angeles, but Chouinard was determined to carry through. That night the detective stationed himself at the backstage door, determined to meet that redhead. Her partner in the act was a pinup girl named Joanne Arnold. He'd discovered Joanne went with a drummer at the Normandy Hotel. When she emerged he walked over to her.

"Hello, Joanne," he said, smiling.

She had never seen him before but apparently thought she had.

"Hi."

"Who's that redhead you're working with? I've never seen her before."

"Paulette."

"I'd like to meet her," he said.

"Come on back. I'll introduce you."

He followed her backstage, met Paulette, and they arranged to have a drink later.

He was doing fine with the two girls when they explained they were going on to Lake Tahoe with the show the next day. Joanne was leaving with her boyfriend early, and she and Paulette were to meet at an intersection fifty miles north.

"Why don't I drive you up to meet Joanne?" he said.

Paulette agreed. He could handle it just right, he assumed. He'd call the Old Man just before he left, drive fifty miles, check in on his hourly call, and then drive back and check in again.

It wasn't to work that way. They missed Joanne at the intersection and found themselves stranded in the desert at a lonely gas station. There was nothing to do but drive Paulette all the way to Tahoe. They started out, got to Tahoe, and he began driving back, afraid to call Hughes for fear the operator would announce it was a long-distance call.

A thousand miles and some fourteen hours later he called The Boss. He knew he had to lie his way out somehow. Also, since it was a Hughes car he had the odometer backed up 1,100 miles.

"Where the hell have you been?" Hughes asked indignantly.

"I had a tip and went out in the desert and passed out," he replied. "I woke up in the emergency room of a hospital."

Hughes paused as Chouinard waited in fear that he'd ask him the name of the hospital.

But Hughes' penchant for detail took another direction. "Don't you have air conditioning in that car?" he demanded.

"No, sir."

There was another long pause. "Well, I'm going to issue a memo that any of our people who use cars out here from now on have to have air conditioning. I was worried about you."

It wasn't all a wasted gesture. A month later Paulette arrived in Los Angeles. Chouinard took her flying and, to impress her, landed the plane on the beach at Malibu to visit Steve, his pal on the Las Vegas trip. Everyone was properly impressed, and the time eventually came when Paulette became Mrs. Chouinard.

CHAPTER 20

AIRPLANES WERE TO REMAIN A FOCAL POINT OF HUGHES' life for decades. Lee Merrin once told Chouinard of Hughes' grandiose plans during the 1930's to build an aircraft barony of his very own. Hughes had bought a great deal of land in Culver City for his plant. He started sketching a project so elaborate that MGM was included in the Hughes daydream.

The youthful billionaire envisioned his own community, which would be in a deep-water port created by dredging La Ballona Creek. He'd have his own runway, aircraft plant, and harbor, where he'd anchor his yacht. His mansion would overlook it all from a high bluff near where Loyola University now stands. It never came to pass, but Hughes was to make the entire U.S. his private airport in a way.

Hughes had planes all over the country, no one knew exactly how many. Like the well-known tale of W. C. Fields, who supposedly secretly opened bank accounts under different names, the Old Man was suspected of having a half dozen planes hidden away at obscure airports under a variety of disguises. His pattern was exactly the same as with girls—he acquired them, used them briefly if at all, then jealously stored them away so no one else could play with them.

The Hughes planes that associates did know about all had guards on twenty-four-hour duty, an expensive undertaking that served no real purpose. One DC-6 at Clover Field in Santa Monica had been bought new and taken off the Douglas assembly line without the interior finished. It stood for fourteen years with around-the-clock guards on duty. Another leased twin-engine Cessna was stored at Lockheed in Burbank and was worth $70,000. Hughes paid lease and storage fees of

$1,700 a month plus hangar fee year after year. Chouinard suggested to Kay Glenn that he'd like to secretly buy the plane and start collecting those fees from Hughes. "If he ever found out about it you'd be in more trouble than you've ever been in," Glenn warned. "If there's anything The Boss hates, it's for his employees to make money off him."

Other aircraft were scattered about the U. S. like toys carelessly dropped by a child. One was in Georgia, another in Wyoming, several at Clover Field, more at Culver City. Another in Arizona. Pilots stood by on alert at some of them. Few of them were ever called.

The DC-6 sat outside on the runway in the salt air at Clover Field, deteriorating for several years. The City of Santa Monica began to pressure Hughes to move the plane because it was in the way of operations. As always Hughes kept stalling.

At one point Maheu was assigned to befriend James Grubbs, a former city attorney for Santa Monica. A deal was struck to lease a big hangar from the city, which would hold at least five planes. The guards were delighted. "Now we'll be inside at night," one said happily.

"Don't get your hopes up," another warned. One guard was sure that the hangar was for the DC-6 and ended up making a five-dollar bet. He lost. The hangar stood empty for years more while the DC-6 remained outside. The simple task of towing the plane inside was more than Hughes could face.

At last the City of Santa Monica decided to act. Officials started badgering Hughes weekly as they wanted to take the hangar back for their own use. They hit upon the device of threatening condemnation because Hughes had made no effort over those years to maintain the building. It was falling apart, they claimed, due to the peeling paint and need for repairs. Hughes got around that by ordering the hangar painted inside and out. It destroyed the basis of any pending legal action.

As the airport became more and more crowded it was an

odd sight to see the huge empty hangar and the DC-6 decaying nearby. At last Hughes tired of the game and gave up the hangar. The plane stayed outside.

He used these planes, test planes, TWA planes, and others with a casualness that constantly created havoc.

At one point he was practicing with an amphibious plane on Lake Mead, near Las Vegas. With him was a mechanic Hughes claimed was a copilot. They'd make regular runs to Phoenix and Los Angeles, always carrying a huge, heavy, coffinlike box on the plane. Hughes insisted it be unloaded at every stop, hauled to his room or wherever he might be staying, and reloaded on the plane the next day. Many observers suspected it was some sensitive electronic gear he was testing.

Then crazy rumors started. It was about the size of a coffin, wasn't it? Was he hauling a body around? Speculation grew until an employee of the Hughes Aircraft Company was unloading the plane one day. He decided to risk all, carefully removed the tape seals, and opened the box. It was filled with hundreds of comic books!

The Old Man, wary as ever of ridicule, didn't want the word to get out that he enjoyed reading comic books before he dozed off.

Later he developed an avid appetite for a certain cookie. This was no commonplace cookie. Hughes had at one point turned his attention to pastry and with his cook Bruno spent some days in Walter Kane's kitchen perfecting the batter. It had been one of those vivid emotional concerns that lasted for weeks as Hughes tasted the amount of cinnamon, sugar, and butter until he felt he'd developed the ideal formula.

From then on the cookies became a serious part of TWA's organizational planning. When Hughes was in Las Vegas, for example, vast machinery would grind. In Los Angeles, Bruno would make a fresh batch and pack them in two or three special round containers. They'd be rushed to the airport by a special driver and delivered personally by the driver to the chief pilot in the TWA flight cabin. He, in turn, would personally carry the sealed and wrapped packages to a waiting driver at the Las Vegas airport. Meanwhile TWA planes going west would reverse the procedure, carrying the wrapped tins back to Los Angeles. If nothing else, it made the captains of those huge planes feel part of something more than just an airline. One of them told Chouinard: "It's secret electronics gear, something to do with space. All very hush-hush. . . ."

Hughes' aides would often get the byplay on such food fetishes through jobs allotted to them. For some years the Old Man was wild about a certain yellow cake. An old lady made the delicacy. He'd receive this coarse-grained and unappetizing-looking cake from the woman each year the day before Christmas. Perhaps she was an old family friend and it was a sentimental gesture for his birthday, December 24. The cake, if nothing else, reminded him of the fact that it *was* his birthday. This may have been the emotional attachment that made the cake such a gourmet delight for him. Whatever, for years on the day before Christmas the old lady would appear at Walter Kane's apartment with the unfrosted cake in a box. Walter would call Hughes with the news and he'd send for it, sit down, and eat the whole cake immediately. While other people opened packages around the Christmas tree, this was Hughes' holiday ritual.

Later, when he'd moved to Bel Air, he arranged to get the recipe from the old lady. He sent it to the chef at the Beverly Hills Hotel, who started making two or three cakes at a time for him. His feeding habits were well established by then. Whatever he was hung up on at the time—candy bars, cake, steaks, beef stew—would be all he'd eat. He'd stuff himself like a lion with a kill, then not eat again for several days.

One day Kay Glenn at Romaine, where the cakes were officially routed on the journey to the Hughes stomach, called Chouinard. Glenn had stolen one! Kay arrived at Chouinard's house for dinner with the cake. They rushed through dinner to get to the epicurean mystery of it all. It was dreadful and seemed to have been made with no sugar. It tasted, as Chouinard described it later, "like stale bread." They each took a few bites and gave up.

At one point when the Old Man was at the Beverly Hills Hotel he conjured up one of his more elaborate dishes. It was a conventional beef stew with one remarkable exception. Each piece of vegetable had to be precisely square and then each corner trimmed off neatly at a forty-five-degree angle. He sent a number of beef stews back when he discovered the corners weren't properly done.

CHAPTER 21

HUGHES' TWIN CHARACTERISTICS OF MEDDLING WITH TRIVIA and procrastinating caused a slowdown in production and put him into serious trouble with the air force at one point after the Korean War. Eisenhower at last sent Secretary of the Air Force Talbot out to see Hughes with an ultimatum. If he didn't quit tinkering and slowing down the production of defense electronics, the government was going to close him down. Both Dr. Woolridge and Simon Ramo, the guiding talents of the Hughes electronics empire, had already quit in frustration.

Hughes used his old methods when he received word that Talbot was arriving. "Put him in the Beverly Hills Hotel," he ordered, "and show him a good time." Hughes had just discovered a new talent and had no time for business.

Talbot, however, didn't want a good time. He wanted action. He also had been briefed on Hughes' stalling techniques. The afternoon he arrived he started raising all hell to see the Old Man immediately.

When Hughes was told, he picked up the phone in his bungalow, a few feet from where Talbot was staying. He was in Houston, he coolly told the Air Force Secretary, and would be in the next day.

The next day he called again. He was having engine trouble. "But I'll be there tonight somehow," he promised. The next morning Talbot packed for Washington and left in a fury. He dictated a written ultimatum. It stated that Hughes was personally to lay off Hughes Aircraft or the air force would take it over. Hughes decided to donate Hughes Aircraft to his medical foundation as profits were small anyway. Later when the income picked up and he needed cash for 707's he was frantic because he couldn't use those Hughes Aircraft profits. This no doubt contributed to his later breakdown.

It was a desperate period. It's inconceivable to most people that a billionaire like Hughes could get down to needing a mere $50,000 in cash, but he reached that moment once. He was financing the purchase of Boeing 707's at the time and had to pay cash in the millions.

Hughes was bewildered that he lacked ready cash. First he called his attorney Chester Davis in New York with an elaborate scheme to take money back from the medical foundation and he was rebuffed because of government regulations. He couldn't understand how the government could be so petty. He eventually sold one of his beloved toys, the DC-6 at Clover Field, which must have cost $1,500,000, to the King of Saudi Arabia for $1,000,000. The deal was quickly struck and he was sent $50,000, with the remainder to be paid on delivery.

Weeks passed. There were polite inquiries from the Mideast

that became more and more firm and frequent. Finally word came that the King wanted his money back. Silence.

Then the Saudi Ambassador went to the State Department. The issue took on diplomatic importance as talk turned to oil and trade agreements. The State Department tried desperately to break through the barriers of the Hughes organization to force the Old Man to do something. "I'll deliver it. I'll deliver it," was his only reply through his chain of command.

At last he was forced to act. He returned the $50,000. The idea of giving up a plane was more than he could face.

The DC-6 continued to sit at the airfield, rusting away. It could easily have been converted into a DC-6B and was a salable item. A group from Wyoming contacted Chouinard. They were ready to spend up to $600,000 for it and put up $125,000 good faith money. Chouinard called the Old Man and told him of the offer but the Wyoming people were not allowed to inspect the plane. Hughes wouldn't even consider it. Moreover, the plane had deteriorated so badly ropes had been put around it; it was guarded night and day so no one could get near it. The deal fell through.

In 1975 an attempt was made to fix up the DC-6 a bit and it was then donated to a non-profit organization.

CHAPTER 22

IN THE EARLY WINTER OF 1951 A MAGIC MOMENT CAME. Gossip and rumors within the Hughes organization proved true: Hughes officially announced a move to Florida, where he was going to settle down permanently and build an aircraft factory.

The great exodus began. Employees took children out of school, sold or leased their homes, and shipped their furniture to Miami. Hughes and his staff moved into a downtown commercial hotel, the Columbus, which everyone soon loathed. Hughes himself lived in a suite, with empty rooms all around him. Chouinard, as a separate contractor, could stay where he pleased. He had no cases to investigate. He chose the Racquet Club on Bay Harbor Island and settled to a leisurely life of swimming, tennis, and drinking. Soon staff members were visiting him every day to escape downtown Miami.

It was here that Chouinard and Glenn were to become close friends. They'd play tennis regularly, then Glenn would accompany Chouinard on a round of nightclub-hopping. The detective was puzzled by this as Glenn, a Mormon, didn't drink but would nevertheless sit with Chouinard for hours, sipping orange juice. The detective knew he was bored and finally asked Glenn why he stayed so close. Glenn confessed. Hughes was fearful that Chouinard might get lonesome or homesick and bolt for California. The detective had already asked to go home for Christmas and Hughes—although he had nothing for Chouinard to do—wanted him to stay. Glenn's mission was to remain close to Chouinard and make sure he didn't leave.

Later, in California, Chouinard and Glenn were to buy a cabin cruiser together. They invited members of the Hughes staff for the maiden voyage and, as they rounded the flying-boat hangar at Long Beach, they spotted Hughes himself standing near the water's edge, chatting with someone. Chouinard started to swing the boat around so all could wave to him. "My God! Don't do that," someone gasped. "If he sees us all together he'll think we're plotting something and we'll be in trouble explaining ourselves!" Still later, when Hughes fired Noah Dietrich, Glenn and Chouinard were to more or less inherit a cabin cruiser twice the size of their boat *Noah's Ark* that was one of the fringe benefits the financial advisor had enjoyed. (A Captain Suggs maintained the new craft. He'd been in charge of the small boats attached to the flying boat. Suggs had been a deep-sea diver after Pearl Harbor and had been hired by Hughes to try to salvage the ill-fated Sikorsky, which had gone down in Lake Mead.)

Hughes' trip to Florida was to turn into a comedy of errors. He had great plans. He was going to build the medical center for his Foundation and created a furor when word got out that he was going to buy one of the big golf courses in Miami for the center. Politicians were in a flurry over the gossip that he planned the aircraft factory near West Palm Beach. It looked like a small Florida land boom again.

Few knew that the great Hughes expedition also involved another of Hughes' prospective girls as a major factor. This one was a bit of a sticky problem, however. She was a movie beauty, but the only daughter of a leading Hollywood director who had a reputation for being rough as a cob and twice as nasty. Hughes had heard tales of him and was wary. The old ploy—the contract, the apartment, the dramatic lessons—certainly wouldn't wash. Hughes plotted a major campaign that was to cost many thousands of dollars. Aides could only marvel at the time at The Boss's raw courage in trying to pull off such nonsense.

It had started with surveillance of the girl's house, a mansion in Beverly Hills on Linden Drive. Problems soon multiplied. The house was a few doors away from the Virginia Hill mansion where the gangster Bugsy Siegel had been shot in the head and not far from where Hughes himself had crashed a plane and nearly been killed. It was a bad area, ripe with the potential for more trouble as any soothsayer could have told Hughes.

Trouble wasn't long in coming. A few nights later there was a murder inside a nearby house—while outside Hughes' men were standing guard. The residents were an old couple, and the woman was found with her head split open by a meat cleaver.

The Beverly Hills police lost no time in calling Chouinard. They'd seen and recognized his stakeout car. Though they didn't actually suspect his men, they wanted to know if the detectives had seen anyone enter or leave the murder victim's house. His men had seen nothing. Chouinard explained their lack of information as best he could to the police. Knowing his men, he didn't feel he could tell the whole truth—that they'd probably been snoozing. A few days before Hughes announced plans to go to Florida, the murder was solved. A cook had become infuriated with the old lady's complaints about an overcooked roast and done the woman in.

Some Hughes people accompanied the girl and her mother on a cross-country train trip. Although Hughes no longer owned RKO, he'd hired an entire movie crew to convince the girl's father that it was a quite legitimate filming trip. Chouinard was aboard to see that no brash movie-crew swain tried to seduce the girl.

The director was a happy cynic about the whole affair. He'd brought a plentiful supply of Scotch and planned to just have fun. He was wrong. The movie crew did get to Orlando and actual shooting of underwater sequences and water skiing got underway. There was constant talk of "shooting around"

Jayne Mansfield, the purported star, until she arrived. Later there was more work at Marathon, but slowly the production efforts dwindled and finally ceased.

Hughes, meanwhile, tried to be a proper escort for the girl despite the continuing search for an aircraft-plant site and the talks over other plans. At one point he rented Gar Wood's yacht and arranged for the actress and her mother to be guests on a morning cruise. "Be prompt," he admonished them. "We're going to leave at ten."

They arrived on schedule to find a frantic Hughes on deck. He'd decided he needed a yachting cap for the outing and had been sending aides to nearby stores for the past hour. They'd rushed back with several dozen caps but the Old Man disliked all of them. One had too much braid, the other was the wrong fabric, and still another had the wrong shape visor. Captain, crew, and guests all waited restlessly on deck as the hunt for the right yachting cap went on. At 1:30 in the afternoon Hughes gave up and ordered the yacht to depart without his cap. There was a short run to sea and the yacht returned. Everyone had a bad day.

For some unknown reason, Hughes' ardent pursuit of the girl ended as quickly as it had begun, as did the movie production, which stopped before it ever really got started. But the Old Man, as usual, still considered the girl his property. When she returned to Los Angeles and started to date Lance Reventlow, the race-driver son of Barbara Hutton, Hughes was properly indignant. He ordered Chouinard to start tailing them on dates. It was hazardous work as Reventlow sped over the freeways of Los Angeles with the girl. After a time the surveillance cars gave up the chase; the drivers complained it was too dangerous. When Reventlow was killed some time later no one was surprised.

Hughes continued to search the Miami area for sites for his plant. What he found in abundance were flies and coral dust.

The end came one late spring when Kay Glenn, driving with Hughes from Broward Field at Fort Lauderdale, took a country road by mistake. The heat was suffocating, particularly as Hughes had ordered all windows closed and sealed with tape to keep out the flies and dust.

Hughes stared balefully at the little swirls of coral dust, sweat pouring down his face. After fifteen minutes of silence he turned to Glenn. "This goddamned Florida dust is worse than the Las Vegas dust. Let's go back to California."

The weary staff began packing once again, taking children out of school, making calls to try to get their houses back. Hughes told some of his staff that he'd fly them back to California, and everyone was mildly concerned. Wild stories of some of the aging Hughes' antics with planes had circulated. But there was nothing to do but agree.

Hughes' own Convair was in San Diego having an overhaul, and the Convair company had lent him a new plane. The reluctant passengers gathered at Fort Lauderdale for the return trip, glancing at the Old Man nervously to ascertain how stable he seemed. Apprehension grew as he walked to the door, gave it a tug, than another, and began to curse.

He fiddled with the lock, called mechanics who tried to open it, and then called more mechanics. Tension grew. By two in the afternoon Hughes was in a rage. He managed to reach the president of Convair at home in San Diego. He angrily demanded to know how to open "the goddamned door."

"That's the new model," the Convair president explained weakly. "I don't know."

More calls were made as the reluctant passengers studied Hughes with growing fear. Eventually the plant foreman was located at a fraternal picnic in San Diego.

At last, at ten that night, Hughes found out how to open the door. By then the courage the staff had tried to build up to fly with the Old Man had faded away. But they took off into the starlit night, hoping they'd somehow land on the other side of the continent. They made it.

CHAPTER 23

WHILE HUGHES COULD BE SHOCKINGLY STINGY ABOUT TRIVIA, he was magnanimous with his favorite toy, TWA. He received endless requests from Cary Grant, Liz Taylor, Eddie Fisher, and many others who were wealthy in their own right for free tickets to New York or for location work. He never failed. They were always accorded the star treatment, with TWA aides on hand to take care of their every want. Although he hadn't seen many of these people for years, it took only a call from a star to the office and the word came back to approve the request.

Cary Grant always remained in Hughes' memory as one of his favorite companions. Years later in Bel Air, Hughes still had his unknown channels of information and would emerge from his apathy if events stirred him sufficiently. When he was told that Cary Grant was ill and in the hospital he immediately called Romaine to order a special motorized hospital bed. When Hughes had crashed and been bedridden, years before, he'd called in an engineer from the aircraft plant who had designed a bed with three units that could be raised and lowered by a small electric motor, a prototype of what was to become a standard hospital bed a few years later. He ordered that such a bed be delivered to Grant. It was, the actor recovered, and the bed was returned to Romaine. Then the Old Man heard of it, and panic came. "Leave it outside," he said. No one must touch it, he ordered, until a plan could be devised. Eventually it was decided that a special room would be cleared for it. An outside workman was hired to move it in and the door was locked. It gathered dust as the deadly germs from the hospital slowly wasted away.

Though generous, Hughes could be cruel and unfeeling, too. Chouinard's wife once met Neil McCarthy, a wealthy old attorney, who lived in a mansion on Sunset Boulevard. He'd been a close friend of Hughes' father, and when the senior Hughes died he'd taken in young Howard, about nineteen at the time, and treated him like a son. Time passed and Hughes moved on. McCarthy said he'd never had so much as a phone call over the years. "I don't even get a Christmas card from him," he added. He wondered why.

Someone mentioned this to Hughes once. "That place always scared me when I was alone," was Hughes' only comment. "It reminded me of a big, haunted house."

Hughes through the years continued to give free rides on TWA to all his friends. His random use of any plane gave him the feeling that he had his own personal air fleet, as indeed he did.

Typically, he'd call Chouinard at home. "I've got a trip for you to take in a half hour," he'd announce. This involved driving some thirty-five miles to the airport—and this was in the days before most of the freeways had been built.

"I'll never make it," the detective would reply.

"Sure you will."

"I have to pack," Chouinard would answer.

"You're wasting time talking. You'll make it."

He'd rush, then drive like hell.

The plane was always there, a big Constellation standing by. The ladder was hauled out and passengers would stare, wondering who he was and why he'd held up the transcontinental flight for a half hour or an hour. It was reportedly illegal, but Hughes did it again and again. No one understood why he made such a game of it. He could have called Chouinard in time. But he enjoyed the suspense.

Hughes had secret sources that kept him informed of TWA goings-on.

At one point he ordered Chouinard's men to start interviewing the parents of a TWA stewardess he suspected might have information she'd sell to Pan Am. No one was sure just what to do when they did talk to her parents, but Chouinard told Bob Roberts, one of his detectives, to simply "play it by ear."

Roberts worked out a unique formula. He bought a dimestore diamond ring and knocked on her parents' door.

The mother answered. "Did anyone lose this ring?" he inquired. "I found it on the sidewalk out in front."

After a bit of chitchat the mother invited him in for coffee. He quickly noticed the picture of the stewardess daughter on the mantel and talked turned to her duties as the proud parents elaborated and gave him all the information he needed.

Such trivia as getting data on what a stewardess might know was commonplace. But in the vast complexities of the Hughes empire there were countless facets that never attracted The Boss's personal interest. There was, for example, no sign that he ever concerned himself with the subtle art of brewing beer, despite the fact that he owned a Texas brewery; but God help the brewmaster if Hughes' attention had suddenly been caught with some detail about the proper yeast content!

At one point, for example, he suddenly sparked to the subject of advertising. Within a few weeks Hughes' advertising personnel, though accustomed to a high-tension profession, knew what real account-executive woes were.

He zeroed in on TWA's ad schedules. The Foote, Cone and

Belding account ran to millions of dollars a year and was a plum for any agency. There already were stories of his dabbling with movie advertising, particularly on *The Outlaw.* Hughes had not only overseen such trivia as all publicity stills but given rapt and particular attention to one huge billboard in Los Angeles, a landmark in the outdoor display industry due to its massive size. He stood by while the sign painters on scaffolds worked. He was pleasant but argued, cajoled, and pleaded that the blouse be lower, lower, and lower until attorneys had to be summoned to explain the billboard laws.

The vice president from the New York agency who arrived in Los Angeles to settle the matter of the multimillion-dollar TWA account renewal was used to dealing big, even if it wasn't with Hughes. But he soon was up against an old Hughes strategy. Each morning the executive would try to arrange a meeting with The Boss and be told to stand by in his room at the Beverly Wilshire Hotel. He waited. Several days passed. Then Hughes called one morning, all easy charm and grace. He explained that he simply couldn't see the man that day and asked what he had to do to keep busy.

The vice president tried to hold down his irritation and said, "Nothing."

"Then can you do me a favor?" Hughes asked.

What account executive wouldn't take bait like that? "Of course, Mr. Hughes."

"There's a young lady living over on Cedarbrook off Coldwater Canyon. If I send a driver and car could you take her to her drama class?"

"Certainly, Mr. Hughes."

"Okay, and then call me when you get her there."

The car arrived, the account executive picked up the girl, delivered her, and called Hughes.

"Would you mind running her on over to her singing class after that?" Hughes asked. It went on all day, to her dancing class, her elocution class, her hairdresser.

The next morning The Boss was on the phone again. Would the account executive mind waiting just one more day?

It lasted for four days. Then the victim exploded. "I'm a top partner and a vice president in my firm and I have a lot of important things to do. I'm not a chauffeur. If you won't see me I'll go back to New York and come back when you can."

Hughes said softly, "You mean you're not going to do it today?"

"No sir! I won't."

"All right," Hughes sighed. "Forget the account and go on back home."

Hughes could show the same infuriating obstinacy in an airplane. There was the time he was toying with a 707 a test pilot had brought him. One night he was coming in at International Airport in Los Angeles. He wasn't in touch with the tower, and the control room kept warning him that he was coming in too low, but he kept going. The test pilot beside him started shouting at him but Hughes refused to listen. At the last moment the test pilot pulled up himself. A huge flap broke off the plane and landed in a drive-in theater but luckily didn't hit any autos. The next day there was a photo in the Los Angeles *Times,* but the story didn't mention who was flying.

Once, Hughes bought a new Constellation that was supposed to go to TWA. After an initial flight he brought it into Lockheed at Burbank and casually pulled it to a position he liked, got out, locked the door, and walked away.

Lockheed operations was on the phone within minutes asking that it be moved, as the area was reserved. Days passed. Then at last Hughes acted. He took off once again for a flight, landed and taxied to a spot where one of the airlines was supposed to unload passengers. He repeated the same performance as before—locked the plane—and departed.

Now Lockheed was in a total uproar. Frantic calls to Romaine got only delaying promises while the Mormons stewed over what to do. Soon Robert Gross, the president of Lockheed, was on the phone, pleading. At last, after two weeks, Hughes gave someone the keys and allowed the plane to be moved.

He had a score of such ways to annoy airfield personnel. One of his favorites was to keep one of his planes at Clover Field; however, as a major source of the field's income was selling gas, he always made it a point to fly the plane to his own field at Culver City to gas up.

If Hughes' petty stunts kept airfield personnel irritated, the Old Man's grander gestures led to true turmoil. One of his finest hours was when he asked Lockheed to lend him a Super Constellation for a test run of a half hour. The brass at Lockheed reluctantly agreed, with the precaution of putting a company representative aboard to "help" him. As Hughes never flew with a copilot, using a mechanic when he had to and claiming the mechanic was the copilot, he agreed easily. The plane, Lockheed pointed out, was due to be delivered to another airline, not TWA, and was spanking new.

Hughes took off, made a long, slow circle, then set out for Montreal, Canada! What conversation he had with the company rep is lost to posterity. He was going there to talk to a British plane manufacturer about buying British planes.

Charging a Cuban refugee with hijacking is one thing. Having Howard Hughes arrested for stealing a Super Constellation is another. Delicate and urgent negotiations began. Hughes, meanwhile, settled in at Montreal. He parked the huge plane at the end of the runway, had an air conditioner installed and made arrangements for someone to come aboard to cook for him. He started sleeping on the plane while his staff stayed at a hotel. When the Lockheed rep tried to plead with him he explained he certainly hoped the rep wouldn't leave, as he needed a technical advisor.

A week later Hughes announced he was ready to take off. Everyone sighed with relief. He took off—and headed for the Bahamas! He'd just leased three islands there from the British and wanted to look them over. It wasn't a spur-of-the-moment decision on Hughes' part. Just before Hughes left, Chouinard had gone to Romaine to get his pay check. He'd been asked to go to the Bank of America branch nearby to get some petty cash for the Old Man. The bank manager was waiting for him and handed him a brown bag. "I can't take this with me without counting the money," the detective said. He opened it and counted off $100,000 in new bills. He tucked the money back in and scurried nervously back to Romaine.

Hughes was to stay in the Bahamas for nearly a month and then suddenly reappear in Los Angeles one day with the corroded plane. Staff members soon heard the gossip of the new personal fetish Hughes had taken up while in the Bahamas. When he'd received his first shipment of Poland water, which he'd ordered after he landed, he started taking enemas with the mineral water. For days he took as many as five enemas daily, then quit abruptly. Hughes complained later that he hadn't liked the Bahamas at all. He didn't trust the colored cooks there and what they might put in the food. It didn't explain the trip. But maybe it did explain the enemas.

CHAPTER 24

AS HUGHES SLOWLY DECLINED, HIS FEW REMAINING BUSINESS efforts were often pathetic. One of the wildest schemes involved buying used four-engine flying boats from World War II. These British-made monsters, battered and beaten for years during the war, had been rusting for some twenty years. But the Old Man had a vision of picking up tourists en route to Lake Tahoe in San Francisco Bay and flying them to the lake, where he could put down on the water.

The ancient flying tubs he envisioned as the backbone of his new airborne fleet would only have been the subject of endless ridicule. Cost surveys showed that it would be much cheaper to build or buy new planes than to try to repair and refurbish these relics. But Hughes was not to be put down.

A vast hush-hush operation started. Chouinard was sent to Hawaii to contact a man who knew of flying boats in New Zealand. Arrangements were made to bring two of the boats across on freighters to the San Francisco airport. Lease space was arranged at Alameda Naval Air Station.

But the final fillip was security. Bill Gay decided that Mormons from Samoa would be the perfect guards for those supersecret planes. As he reasoned, they'd not only be as sober and serious as native Mormons but would be strangers in a strange land. The lures of San Francisco would not attract them.

With the planes in place a unique contingent of security guards arrived: four husky Polynesians, who gawked with awe and bewilderment at the skyscrapers and wonders of the Bay area. Meanwhile aircraft engineers came to study the huge flying boats, shook their heads in despair, and departed. Tensions increased as executives were pressured by the Old Man, who wanted action and progress reports daily.

As for the guards, they were a sociological study in what can happen to Samoan village lads in a big city. They soon discovered the tawdry lures of North Beach's gin mills, whores, strip joints, and lowlife. Most of them were drunk at any given time. They wandered off from their post or stretched out on the asphalt and went to sleep. Some disappeared for days on end. Within a few weeks they were ordered to bundle up their things and go back to Samoa to resume the quiet life.

A new platoon of guards was sent from Romaine. Hughes complained about the Samoans—and Mormons at that!—being demoralized by booze. This attitude toward strong drink was typical. He sipped rum and Cokes, or rum highballs, with companions in his early days and showed no prejudice against such drinking. But when alcohol obstructed his plans it was another matter. He seemed to be able to tell if an associate had been imbibing when he talked with him on the phone. He'd never accuse anyone directly of having a snootful but ordered some immediate chores, which would end the fun.

Indeed, Hughes himself once had a barroom brawl in the 1940's, when he was practicing landings with his Sikorsky amphibian on Lake Mead. He'd stopped for a few drinks with a few assistants at the Fremont Hotel in downtown Las Vegas. When it was time to pay he accused the bartender of short-changing him ten cents. The barkeeper wouldn't budge. Hughes reached across the bar, grabbed the bartender by the shirt, and was trying to punch him when his assistants pried him loose.

Nearly lost in the mist of the Hughes legend is an incident from the 1920's when Hughes and a companion devised a youthful adventure. It shows his interest in girl-collecting as a hobby was already in full bloom.

Hughes and his pal, traveling under aliases, set off on a junket in a rickety car, heading east from Texas. They carried with them a professional portrait camera and a satchel of greenbacks. At small towns across the South they'd settle in and put an ad in the local paper, announcing they were big-shot Hollywood photographers and were searching the hinterlands for star material for a film studio. Mothers would arrive with their pretty daughters, and the youths would take pictures, promising that the girls would hear from Hollywood soon.

They worked their way as far east as Alabama and started a tour back. Only tabloid stories that young Hughes was missing and might have been kidnapped ended the spree when the two youths were apprehended in Louisiana.

It was the forerunner of dozens of episodes to come. One of Hughes' finest misadventures was to come when he became fascinated with the photos of a French ballerina, Jeanmaire. She was beautiful and lithe, with the long, agile legs of a dancer. Hughes was beside himself with excitement and dispatched an envoy to call on her in France with the usual offer of a movie contract. It was to no avail. Not only was she under contract to the Ballet de Paris—its star as a matter of fact—but inordinately loyal to her troupe.

The Old Man was not easily put aside in such matters. He told Walter Kane to hire the entire troupe, bring it to Los Angeles, and start seeking bookings. Kane was bewildered but did manage to complete a contract to import the ballet troupe. Then the trouble started. Signing a starlet and putting her in a movie of some sort was one thing for Kane but being an impresario in the arts and selling culture was an entirely different bag. He made a few awkward efforts to line up engagements but gave up in despair when Hughes added another qualification. Jeanmaire was not to appear with the troupe but stay in Hollywood with Hughes. Without the star, only one brief engagement, a token effort, was arranged and then the troupe of twenty settled in at the Château Marmont to relax and enjoy sunny California on the RKO payroll.

The days stretched into weeks as Hughes tried with growing frustration to woo the lovely dancer. To complicate the romance, she spoke no English. Hughes disappeared at one point for four days with French grammar books and recordings, for a crash course in French. When he emerged he was able to have some rudimentary conversation with the girl.

This only made things more annoying. The dancer was pleasant, cheerful, and fun-loving but viewed the billionaire as an aging and amusing eccentric. She'd smile, laugh, and giggle at "Papa," as she called him, while he tried to court her. The expenses continued to soar and there were restless stirrings among stockholders at RKO who'd heard of the venture. To Jeanmaire it was all a wonderful joke.

Desperate, Hughes simply took off and disappeared. The troupe was told to pack and go back to France, and the dancer later married the troupe's director, Roland Petit.

But the stockholders didn't forget. They were to complain about it for years.

Failures in these frantic excursions into romance were bad enough. But nothing so fragmented the Hughes psyche as publicity about such personal and delicate matters.

At five one afternoon a red alert sounded from Romaine as executives were called and told to stand by for an emergency operation. A clerk whispered to Chouinard, "There's a new issue of *Confidential* out with a story about the Old Man. The shit is hitting the fan."

Chouinard went to the corner drugstore and bought the new issue of the scandal sheet. He read it several times, pondering over what the big stir was about. It seemed generally harmless, full of vague innuendo but with nothing really new. There were all the old tales about The Boss and the actresses he'd escorted over the years, his eccentricities and odd ways.

But after a few Hughes phone calls he realized the Old Man must be planning something comparable to the Normandy invasion. The detective was asked how many friends he could muster to work that night. Chouinard replied perhaps fifteen. A few minutes later he was called back to ask if he couldn't get at least fifty, with cars of their own. He said he'd try.

"What's this all about?" he asked. He was told curtly that he'd be told his assignment but to get hopping in lining up his "team."

By seven that evening Chouinard's orders had come through. The mission: to blanket the Los Angeles area and buy up every copy of the new issue of *Confidential.* He was ordered to Romaine Street to get a bagful of cash and be given a map with assigned sectors of the city. He was then to muster his team, give them the money, and set to work.

It seemed an impossible task to Chouinard. He riffled hurriedly through the classified phone directory, looking at the hundreds of grocery stores, drugstores, newsstands, and liquor stores that would be likely to sell magazines. Then he multiplied by ten for the places that weren't in the book. The best he could hope to do was fan out his team in the assigned area and scour the streets for likely outlets.

By nine o'clock he, bar pals, relatives, and anyone he could find were in battle formation and set to work, two-man teams driving from one store to the next. One man rushed in, bought the copies available, threw them in the back of the auto, and then they drove on, looking for the next likely target.

Many hundreds of men worked to make a dent in the supply spread across the vast area. They kept on for hours as the detective drove about, contacting his team when he could spot them and giving them more cash. By two in the morning they'd done all they could and cars were filled with stacks of the magazines.

At a prearranged dump spot some of the vast army arrived and unloaded the magazines. Chouinard could only estimate the great pile at perhaps a hundred thousand copies. But what fascinated him was the people who had been assigned to this frenetic mission. He had never had a clear picture of the scope of the Hughes power base. There were dozens of faces he'd never seen. Many of them had to be from cells of different parts of the vast Hughes empire, to have been mustered so rapidly. Like Chouinard's own team, maybe most were people who'd been hastily recruited. That left several hundreds who were on a regular Hughes payroll somewhere and had been called for this great overnight crusade. It was a display of immediately available power such as he'd never seen. They arrived, dumped the magazines, and drove away. The operation was, over all, a success, although a few pockets remained the next morning, as cleanup crews swept the city once again to pick up the remaining copies. The next time Chouinard got a call for an assignment there was no mention of the incident; his job was to check on activity at the house of one of Hughes' girls.

Only once again was he alerted to the possibility of another operation of such scope. It was when the book *The Carpetbaggers* was released. Chouinard received word that Hughes was annoyed about his resemblance to one of the characters. While it actually wasn't a clear portrait of Hughes, people thought it was. There was the likelihood that they'd have to buy up all the copies in bookstores. For some reason it never came off. Hughes executives were sent, however, to try to shelve the movie. That, too, failed somehow and the picture was made.

CHAPTER

25

HUGHES HAD HIS OWN PREFERENCES IN GIRLS. HE FAVORED brunettes, and he liked them as young as fifteen if possible. Perfect breasts and long legs were among his mild fetishes but not a necessity. He made no kinky demands but was quick to become bored after a conquest.

The elaborate and detailed games he played before he made his kill were apparently as exciting to him as the thrill of the hunt is to any other sportsman. There was, too, his pride in the trophy. In his later years, when he sat for endless hours watching old movies on television, he'd call one of his sickbed aides when a girl appeared on the scene.

"Remember her?" he'd ask Johnny Holmes with a smile. Old drivers—then practical nurses—said these occasions were the times he showed a sort of sense of humor.

No one at Romaine or elsewhere was clear where the girls all came from and—as they had strict orders never to converse with them about personal matters—they seldom had any way of finding out. Hughes had people spotted across the country who, either for a bounty-hunter fee or simply to curry favor with him, recruited these girls. Some knew of one: Jimmy Vernon, who had once owned the Club La Martinique in New York City and was always on the Hughes payroll in Las Vegas until he died in 1976. Jimmy was constantly on the prowl. His technique was to cruise Las Vegas bars until he came across a likely prospect. If Hughes was in town, he'd call him. Sometimes Hughes would fly from Los Angeles. He'd hurry by, walk through the bar, and give Jimmy the nod or reject. The girl would never know. If Hughes was interested, Vernon would approach the girl and use the hoary gimmick of asking her if she was interested in a screen test. If so, Jimmy would immediately make arrangements, charter a private plane, and send her on her way, after calling a Hughes security man to have him tail her from the airport. A bugged suite in a fashionable hotel would be ready. The task of surveillance would start, gathering data on whom she saw, whom she phoned, what she did. After a few days Hughes would ask for "the script on that girl Jimmy sent over last week."

Hughes himself was also endlessly on the hunt, through periodicals. Chouinard remembers being called once to talk of a security matter. Hughes had a copy of *Life* on his lap. It was graduation time and there was a photo of a Mills College girl in cap and gown on the cover. The detective paid little attention to it at the time. A week later the girl was in Los Angeles and under his surveillance.

Hughes would tear pictures out of all sorts of magazines and newspapers. Hughes once dispatched Christy Shepherd, his full-time photographer, to Florida to photograph a girl who'd won some sort of fishing tournament and whose picture had appeared in an outdoors magazine. Christy always methodically followed the Hughes dictum: a profile shot, a full-face shot without makeup or lavish hairdo, and one body shot in plain clothes. These studies naturally tended to look more like police-lineup pictures than girlie photos, but Hughes apparently reasoned that he wanted to first see the girls as plain and drab as possible to get a perspective on what they would look like when glamorized. The Florida fishing-contest winner was sheer tragedy. She'd been shot at an interesting angle for the photo in the magazine. What Christy brought back were stills of a pockmarked, homely, freckled girl grinning at the camera with two teeth missing in front. Hughes took one look, grunted, and threw them aside. But at Romaine Street the photos became objects of derision and amusement for days.

Chouinard once asked Christy how many pictures he'd

taken over thirty years. He was a loyal and secretive man. "Hundreds?" he was asked.

"Thousands," was his only reply.

No one knows the secrets of the files at Romaine Street. There are steel cabinets filled with, indeed, thousands of Christy's pictures of anonymous women. Most of them would be amazed to know they were the object of Hughes' interest at some point over the years.

Hughes thought nothing of dispatching Christy any place in the world on such assignments. Once he came across a photo of Sophia Loren in a fan magazine before she was known as a star. Christy took off immediately for Rome, got pictures of her, and was back in a few days. Hughes didn't like her nose, but he sent for her, put her in the Château Marmont on Sunset Strip for a time. She soon left.

Christy told intimates that he always had to maintain the illusion that he believed Hughes was really looking for girls for movies, although they both knew the hypocrisy of the myth. Once Christy made a nearly fatal error when he was sent to Merced, California, to get the usual pictures of some girl. He arrived on her wedding day and called Hughes to inform him.

"I don't give a goddamn what day it is," Hughes said. "Get the pictures anyway. She might be star material." By then perhaps Hughes had been at the game for so long he didn't realize his own real motivation any longer.

Take 1955, a vintage year for the Hughes vineyards. Somehow the Old Man was not to taste the sweet wine of his crop, however, due to his usual meddling and procrastination. Still it was a lively time, with an array of beauties coming and going. Surveillance men and detectives were busy with the newcomers in addition to the regular list of Hughes girls.

In February a brown-haired beauty with green eyes, whom we shall call Miss Chablis, appeared. She was about eighteen, had won a beauty contest in the East, and had somehow found her way to a shabby, rented house in North Hollywood, when she was called to Hughes' attention. Alas, her dream was destroyed before it really began. Hughes ordered an immediate investigation. Within a few days it was discovered she was living with a grizzled sixty-five-year-old Western actor who played a chuckwagon cook in a television series. The Old Man was so outraged at her peculiar tastes that he dropped her as a prospect immediately.

Next came Miss Sparkling Burgundy, a magnificent, blue-eyed, twenty-year-old brunette with porcelain skin, whom one guard described as having the face and figure "Liz Taylor probably wished she had." Her curious problem was that she lived with her father, a retired businessman, who had only one dream in life—to build his own boat. The Old Man put him on the payroll right away and set him to work constructing a ketch in the back yard. But while Hughes dillydallied, a Los Angeles news commentator spotted Miss Sparkling Burgundy and set her up in her own apartment. The Old Man yelled foul, but it was too late. The commentator, who specialized in bleating about motherhood, old-fashioned decency, and the like, had pirated the prize. Hughes took the father off the payroll.

In May, Hughes himself was to spot a beauty of about nineteen we'll call Miss Muscatel, waiting for a bus at the juncture of Sunset Boulevard and Sunset Plaza. He called Chouinard and ordered a full investigation. A man was put on surveillance for some days but the girl failed to appear. A nearby photography-shop owner was solicited to help out. He eventually spotted her and called Chouinard. Investigation showed she was a part-time UCLA student and apparently respectable. The old saw of the movie contract was arranged. Surveillance showed she had no dates or other evil habits. Her one recreation was to strike out at four in the morning for San

Pedro, where she'd go aboard her father's small cabin cruiser and take out to sea for a morning cruise. This seemed innocent enough until the surveillance men came across the awful truth. She had a boyfriend who was getting aboard before she arrived and coming up on deck and leaving after she had departed. When Hughes heard he was being hoodwinked in such a style her contract was canceled immediately.

The next find was referred to by the detectives as "The little Irish girl." Hughes again had seen her driving by in a car and taken the license number. Chouinard's follow-through showed she lived in a poor section of East Los Angeles. A Hughes aide went to the house and offered a routine screen test. But before anything developed a shocking, typed note arrived at Romaine. "Hughes, if you don't lay off that little Irish girl you're going to end up dead."

Chouinard was given the note with orders to find who sent it. He took it to a documents expert in Los Angeles, the man who proved that the Lindbergh kidnapping ransom note was written by Bruno Hauptmann. The paper was not slick enough to pick up fingerprints but the expert was able to give the year and model of the typewriter used.

Meanwhile, it was discovered the girl had a boyfriend who was extremely jealous. He worked at a service station. A man was sent to get a tuneup and casually asked the owner of the station if he had a typewriter, as he wanted to address an envelope and get it in the mail. The owner motioned inside the station and the typewriter proved to be the same as the one the threatening note had been typed on. Hughes then arranged for a police detective to visit the youth and frighten him with the threat of jail. Hughes, however, dropped the girl immediately.

Such mail was not uncommon. Once Chouinard was called when a package that made a ticking noise arrived at Romaine. As it was before the time of street radicals, Chouinard opened it without further ado. It contained a cheap clock. Another suspicious package proved to contain a mechanical tarantula that leaped out when the lid was taken off the box.

Crank mail was another matter. One woman, who was apparently slightly mad, wrote twice a year. The envelope would always contain a half dozen religious pictures and a note saying she was about to leave on an ocean voyage but would pray for Hughes always and hope he was in good health.

Another always addressed her letters to Howard Hughes, Jr. She was under the impression that she'd given birth to a son by Hughes, and had named him Junior. She believed Hughes was keeping the boy and would send cheap toys and candy at Christmas and Easter. Through the years this went on as if the boy always remained the same age.

Blatant offers from girls of all shapes and sizes weren't uncommon. Typically, one letter from Belgium written in French was given to Chouinard to translate. Enclosed were two nude photos of a beautiful girl. The letter was formal and polite, from a boyfriend. He outlined the girl's talents as a singer, dancer, and acrobat and offered her to Hughes. It was arranged that the Old Man never saw the photos and letter.

Out of the endless quest for girls would emerge a girl who would become a real project for the Hughes forces. Perhaps a fair estimate is that one out of a hundred who were investigated or photographed was contacted. Romaine aides were then to get the girl settled, often with her mother, start collecting data on her through wiretaps and surveillance, and build a file. If she had a boyfriend, as most such beautiful girls did, aides had to devise a plan to sever that tie.

Miss Riverside, as we shall call her, was to become the horror of the whole Hughes structure for nearly five long years. She started out as a commonplace enough subject, a long-limbed, raven-haired girl of fifteen who'd won the title of Miss Riverside in a beauty contest in California a few months before. Hughes probably saw her photo in a newspaper. The first word came with a call from Romaine Street. She and her mother were moving into the Beverly Hills Hotel the next day and she was to go under routine surveillance.

Hughes' machinery moved in to start the "star" buildup. Mother and daughter were whisked by limousine through smart shops for a new wardrobe. Schedules were coordinated for photographs, hair styling, makeup studies, drama classes, vocal tutoring, and a variety of interviews with talent-department bosses and directors.

Within the week it was quite clear to Miss Riverside's mother—a plain little housewife—that she was a fifth wheel. When it was politely suggested by her daughter that she go home she was the first to understand.

Meanwhile Chouinard moved into the room next to the girl and started accumulating a file by listening to calls, checking her mail when she was gone, and collecting reports on her idle conversation.

One salient fact emerged. She had a boyfriend and, although she'd been told to break off all ties and devote herself solely to her career, she had made arrangements to meet him on the sly. It had already happened once. He'd driven to Los Angeles, parked on a side street near the hotel, and she'd sneaked out of the room at 2 A.M. They'd driven to a vacant lot and parked until 3:14 A.M. and then he'd dropped her off.

This was reported to Hughes. "Break it up right now," he ordered.

The next week a bugger tapped in on the call from Miss Riverside's boyfriend and heard a late-hour rendezvous being arranged. Chouinard called the hotel's house detective, and the two men picked up the boyfriend on Crescent Drive, where he sat parked, awaiting Miss Riverside. The house detective gruffly ordered him to get out. Chouinard and the house detective frisked him, then took him to the basement of the hotel. The poor kid was white with fear.

"We're going to turn you in to the police," Chouinard said.

"We've been watching you and know you've been parking here for the last couple of weeks."

The boy asked timidly why that was wrong.

"There have been three robberies in the last week in this hotel," the house detective announced accusingly.

As the boy started to plead his innocence they took his wallet and scribbled down his identification. "I just came to visit my girlfriend," he said, near tears by now. "She's studying here and she's going to be a star. But if they find out I'm seeing her it will ruin everything."

They made a deal. "We don't believe your story," Chouinard told him, "and we have your name and address. You look like a suspect to us. But if we never see you around here again, we'll forget about you."

That was the last time they heard of him.

The slow processing of the girl went tediously on. She continued to try to call her boyfriend. He wouldn't come to the phone. Her lessons left her exhausted. Staff members took her out to dinner. She still didn't know who her producer was. It was part of the programming to let her become lonely and frustrated, desperate for excitement while she was being kept prisoner even though she didn't realize it.

Surveillance can be the most boring of chores when there's nothing happening. One day the detective went into the girl's room when she was at her vocal lesson and drilled a small hole beneath the doorknob connecting his room with hers. Then Chouinard took the brass plate off his side of the door. He had a view of most of the room. He did this simply as a precautionary measure at the time, thinking he'd be ready if any crisis came.

Then late one afternoon he heard the stereo turned up high.

He went over to see what was going on. If he'd had any question of the narcissistic drives of would-be stars he had confirmation before him. Miss Riverside had stripped down and was dancing nude before the mirror to amuse herself. The idea of seeing Hughes' future mistress in the buff before the Old Man did pleased him. He couldn't resist calling in several of the Hughes drivers to give them a turn watching the daily spectacle. They'd sit with drinks chortling over how they'd sort of cuckolded The Boss.

Hughes was, all this time, in a room directly across the hall. It was a month before the girl was told she was under contract to him. She still hadn't seen him. Then he made his move. He called her from those few feet away and explained that he was in New York and would be flying in. "One of these nights we'll have dinner," he said.

She was beside herself with excitement. She had received a call directly from Howard Hughes. Long distance besides!

He started calling her each evening. "I'm in Denver and as soon as the weather clears I'm going on to Houston, then I'll be in Los Angeles," he'd explain.

The tension grew for nearly a week in this manner. Then the great day arrived. Hughes called Chouinard to his room across the hall. "I won't need you anymore on this," he said. "Pack up and get out this afternoon."

Chouinard officially checked out. Then he couldn't resist. He returned to the room, turned on the listening devices, and sat there awaiting the Hughes preview. He had to watch him operate.

About seven Hughes rapped on her door. He introduced himself, apologized for his irksome delays in reaching Los Angeles, and complained about all his business problems. The awestruck girl was all sympathy. They left for dinner in one of the limousines that, naturally, wasn't his as the Romaine Street operation had borrowed it to "try out" from a dealer.

Two hours later they were back in the room. The stereo went on with soft music.

Chouinard then listened with amazement as a new facet of this peculiar man was revealed. For nearly half an hour they chatted of different pop singers, and Hughes animatedly expanded on the weaknesses and assets of an array of pop singers, hippie composers, and guitar players. This most private of the world's famous men, who seemed never to know what day it was or even what decade he was living in, could chat in the fan-magazine lingo of the teen-ager!

The rest was anticlimax. There was a long silence, the stereo was turned off as well as the lights . . . and they were in bed.

Another conquest was completed.

CHAPTER 26

SEVERAL WEEKS LATER MISS RIVERSIDE WAS MOVED TO AN apartment and a bit later to a small house with a maid on Cambria near UCLA. (I mention this street name because as girls were shifted their names changed; surveillance men always used their locale as the code name for them. "Cambria came out of the house and chatted with the mailman and was given three envelopes," a surveillance man would report. Others would know then when they checked the house for letters if she'd hidden one away. Again a stakeout would call in, "Beverly Hills Bungalow Four was in the lobby, went to the cigarette counter, and is now back in her quarters.")

Miss Riverside, as I'll continue to call her, presented only one major problem in the beginning. After returning from her days of lessons, for relaxation she'd take long walks in the evening. She'd wear out the operatives who tried to keep up with her long strides. To add to their concerns the maid—a

Hughes plant from Romaine Street—was giving them added headaches. She kept claiming that Riverside was "getting zingy-zingyed," as she called it, by someone. After reporting this directly to Romaine Street she'd explain she could tell by "her panties." No one could understand either how this "zingy-zingy" was happening or how the maid could tell by her panties, but the news was quickly relayed to Hughes.

He was indignant. "Jesus, Jeff, how can this happen? Don't the men stay with her? Or maybe it's one of our own men."

"No!" Chouinard said. "Absolutely no! She doesn't go anywhere except for those walks and we always tail her then. And I know our own men couldn't be touching her."

It was finally decided by all that they were dealing with a kookie maid, who felt she had to report something sensational to keep her job. By now everyone had real concerns about this Hughes-Miss Riverside affair. For as the years passed it was obvious the girl was not just another specimen in the harem. Hughes was really fascinated with her. To add to the complications she cursed and browbeat him mercilessly. He almost seemed to enjoy being the object of her contempt. The detectives would often listen in on the phone taps when she was on a rampage, then tell the others.

"You dirty old son of a bitch," she'd yell. "You never come to see me. I'll bet you can't even get it up anymore! You're nothing but a decaying old turd . . ." The vile tirade would go on and on while he'd try to placate her.

Then the time came that Hughes seriously started working on the girl's career. He'd call Chouinard about her almost daily, although he only saw her perhaps once a month. He seemed to be sure she'd been faithful, despite the upsetting charges of the maid. To calm her, he told her he was going to have her cut a record that would make her a famous singer.

When he made such a commitment Hughes always did things in the grand manner. He rented a studio and technicians, hired Manny Harmon and his orchestra, and Miss

Riverside cut the record. Disc jockeys at every available radio station were paid off to play it a certain number of times a day. Her albums mysteriously went into the windows of every major music-store window.

It was a fiasco. Her voice was high-pitched and truly dreadful. One couldn't tell if she was trying to be an opera or pop singer. Disc jockeys, even though they'd been paid, would laugh openly on the air after the record had been played. Comics made jokes about it.

Walter Kane, who'd been personally assigned by Hughes to the job of organizing the enterprise, took to drinking heavily. One night, when the derision was at its peak and Hughes mercilessly chopped Walter apart for his failure to make Miss Riverside a pop star, one of the detectives, Bob Roberts, was sitting with Walter as he belted down Scotch highballs and bemoaned his fate. Suddenly he called Manny Harmon and asked him to join them.

When Manny came, Walter put on the record. The whine came billowing out of the speaker. "Bob, what do you think of that?"

Bob was too embarrassed to comment. "Well, it's . . . it's . . . " he stammered.

"It's shit!" Walter cried. "Complete shit, shit, shit!" He pointed at Manny Harmon. "And it's all his fault!" he ranted. "This is the guy who did it all—not me."

Then Walter went wild. He began pulling drapes off the window, tore his shirt to tatters, and howled, while Manny and Bob sat petrified by the tantrum. Bob eventually calmed him down and got him to bed.

Soon after, the girl was moved to Coldwater Canyon. By now she was bitter and suspicious. She began open warfare with the surveillance crew, reporting to Hughes that the men were harassing her during the long walks. He in turn would denounce them because they weren't stealthy enough. Efforts were made to use a series of new youths and rotate them to avoid detection. Surveillance cars were parked at different spots. But nothing would work. She'd keep Hughes and Romaine Street in a constant uproar with her complaints and cursing denunciations. Then a young guard suggested a possible solution.

He discovered that by going to the top of Franklin Canyon on the opposite side of the hill the crew could look directly down at Miss Riverside's house.

They started out by putting two men on the hill. But the men complained it was cold and dark and they were afraid of wild animals. So arrangements were made to construct a simple foxhole with two-way radios, a camper stove for hot coffee, and all the other little comforts of home.

That wasn't enough for the brave novice Sam Spades. To get to the top of the mountain they had to pass some beehives and were afraid they might be stung, and they continued to complain about the possibility of wild animals such as coyotes or wildcats. The climax came when one of the sleuths saw a rattlesnake and, in the excitement, tripped and broke his ankle. Then he couldn't leave well enough alone but filed for Workmen's Compensation. Chouinard had a low insurance rate, as the cover was that these men did nothing but check credit. "What are these men doing on the top of a hill stepping on rattlesnakes?" an insurance investigator asked.

"It was a very unusual case," Chouinard explained.

Yet the foxhole was ideal as a command station. The girl's complaints had stopped and Hughes wasn't calling. Chouinard's men could survey everything and radio to the stakeout men and autos when the girl emerged so they could fade away and she'd never see them.

They slowly expanded the observation point, covering it, then rented a bulldozer and started cutting a road up to the foxhole through the scrub brush. Someone called the owner of the property, who appeared and wanted to know what was going on. He was told that they were just building a fire road.

He was most grateful. Then observers in a sheriff's helicopter saw men at work on the road, got a license number when one of them left work, and called him. The sheriff's office had to be told a surveillance was going on. They let things continue but started watching regularly.

A new situation developed soon after when John Raitt, the singer, who lived nearby, started improving his property. His family apparently had given him a small tractor as a present and he began digging away at the mountainside brush where the eagle's nest was perched. Each day he'd emerge and chew away more and more scrub brush. The surveillance crew knew they'd soon be exposed. Someone suggested some voodoo. The crew killed the next rattler they came across and put the dead reptile on the tractor seat. Raitt stopped work after that.

A new problem emerged. The sheriff's office called. "Is one of your men named Jim Manino and was he on shift working for you in Franklin Canyon last night?"

Chouinard replied he was.

"Does he usually strip down and take a nude girl with him when he works up there?" the deputy asked sarcastically.

The brave little band really didn't hold up too well in the war with that girl. The detectives just weren't born to be paramilitary leaders. One ex-marine from Georgia was put in a surveillance car. When he'd check in at the foxhole he'd sign off with "ten four." The first few times everyone was puzzled. Then they became annoyed. Chouinard thought maybe he was giving the address on the street where he was parked and finally asked another man in the foxhole, "What the hell does that four ten or ten four mean?"

"That's police lingo for ending a conversation," he explained. Chouinard recalls he wondered once again why he had become a detective.

Although Miss Riverside couldn't spot the men, she knew

they were still around. That seemed to annoy her even more. While she was giving the frightened folk at Romaine Street fits about a variety of other things by phone and continuing to denounce the Old Man as an impotent slob, she seemed to be stalking men in surveillance autos as a pastime. As they were being paid to stalk her, this hardly seemed fair.

One day, she sneaked out for a walk and took a side street. She found one bored driver snoozing in his auto. Stealthily she reached in and stole the car keys and began to run. The superspy awakened and started chasing her. He caught her, threw her to the ground, took the keys, cursed her, and left. Naturally, he didn't tell anyone. He apparently was afraid he'd be fired.

Some twenty minutes after the incident Chouinard got a frantic call from Romaine Street. "What's going on up there?" the man on duty shouted. "The Old Man just called and he's really hopping mad. That broad just called and said one of your men beat her up!"

"That's ridiculous!"

"Well, she told The Boss she has bruises to prove it."

Chouinard denied all. The next day he found out it was true.

If Chouinard had muddled through up until now, the bitter climax was to come only a few days later.

One of his crew of stalwarts—a college goof who was a family friend of his wife—stood up in the foxhole in a white t-shirt to survey the house with binoculars. What he saw was Miss Riverside on the patio looking back up at him with a pair of binoculars!

Chouinard thought he had enough trouble, then new complications arose. Some weeks before, his wife had insisted he hire a family friend, a UCLA student. As he was short of men he put him on the crew keeping surveillance on Miss Riverside and forgot about him.

It turned out the youth had secretly been going to the house at night and throwing pebbles at her window, trying to talk with her. She had said nothing, then suddenly called Hughes. Hughes called Romaine Street in one of his rages. Chouinard was contacted. As he knew nothing about it he could only deny everything again and complain that Miss Riverside was simply trying to make more trouble for the security people.

Although he was able to pacify everyone concerned, he had an uneasy feeling about this newcomer who was untested in the field.

Then a few nights later when she was talking with Hughes on the phone the errant young detective sneaked to her front door and rang the bell. She told Hughes to wait on the phone and answered the door. Hughes heard their conversation. Now the Old Man knew it was true! He was furious. He sent word he was pulling Chouinard's men off the job and replacing them with a Mormon accountant from Romaine Street. It seemed as though Chouinard was through.

Chouinard cornered his wife's recruit, the little son of a bitch who'd done this. He'd presumed, of course, that the young man was simply trying to bed the girl down. The youth admitted he'd been trying to see her. But his reason left Chouinard stunned. He wanted to save her—this brittle little chippie—from becoming a fallen woman! "She deserves to have a home and family," he told the detective.

Chouinard fired him, naturally. The gallant lad said it would make no difference. He was going to continue to protect her and save her.

I quote from a phone message from Hughes which explains not only Hughes' fury but other things, his confusion between the identity of "Jeff" and "Mike," the way the unctuous Mormon clerks substituted such words as *intercoursing* and *Eternal Spirit* for words Hughes had used that offended them.

This is Hughes at that stage in his life when he was beginning to slip into his dark madness.

> Tell Bill that, as usual, I've spent 20 minutes of frustrated intercoursing around on the phones before I've come to the conclusion that I can't reach him and that he's not at home and that Hollywood number doesn't answer either, etc., etc., etc., and I wish you would tell Bill that I thought with this situation of this man that gave us the trouble at the Coldwater party's house still open and pending and no action apparently being taken to prevent this thing occurring aagin tonight I thought he would remain at home to discuss the matter and I'm very disappointed that he didn't. Therefore, since I am not able to talk to him about it I will leave it to him to take some action to see that the matter does not reoccur tonight, that the emissary that Jeff sent to talk to this man is completely untrustworthy and the entire conversation has been related back to the Coldwater party in every detail so obviously nothing further should be done through that channel. If Bill and Jeff are unable to find some way to prevent Mike's ex-employee from going on our property I'll find a way to prevent it. I'd like Bill to do something about it and do it in time to prevent a reoccurrence of this thing tonight and if he doesn't by Heavenly Father I will. Well, you might tell him this, if he and Jeff are unable to find a way to prevent this man from making any further trouble and talking to this girl and inciting her to distrust me and everybody else here, in other words, if they are unable to prevent an ex-employee of Mike's from causing the kind of trouble that this man is causing with this girl not only by seeing her in the middle of the night by stirring her up and inciting her distrust in me and blaming Jeff and everything and so forth and so on then I don't want anything further to do with Mr. Conrad and I want to discharge him and his people immediately. If they can't find a way to handle this guy so that he does not make any further attempt to contact this girl and he's got her phone number incidentally, and if they can't find a way to do that, either by phone or in person then I want Jeff laid off as of at once and all of his men and want nothing further to do with them if they can't deliver a little better service than this. I don't want anything further to do with him. This man also happens to be the man who for 9 months

betrayed our trust in him up at or near the Veteran place—the man that Jeff so stupidly sent to try and talk to this man and I suppose persuade him to leave this girl alone and find out what this is all about—is the man that we have been seeking all this time and who I understood from Bill had been discharged long ago and was no longer around. If he still isn't on the payroll he is still a very close friend of Jeff's and this is the man who betrayed us for 9 months at the other house up there, up near Veteran. So, I mean this all just adds up to the fact that this Jeff is doing the dumbest, most incompetent, clumsy operation that I've ever run across and it appears to me that they are about as much responsible for the trouble with this girl as any other single factor and if they can't find a way to throw the fear of God into this miserable bastard that is going up there ringing this girl's doorbell at 2 o'clock in the morning, if they can't find a way to handle this guy, physically or by way of scaring the shit out of him, then I just don't want anything more to do with Jeff or any of his people and would like them laid off immediately. Tell that to Bill. Tell him that I think that he was really very inconsiderate to leave his home tonight with this thing open and without getting it settled one way or the other.

Chouinard assumed that he was through and sat back to await notice. Then he received word that he was to deliver a message to the would-be savior of innocent women. It had apparently been written by the Old Man in his rage. It read:

If you were a free agent you could do whatever you pleased and no one would give a damn, but you are not. You took his money and you worked for him in a fiduciary capacity and you worked for him in a position of trust. When you took the position, you agreed to this trust. What you are doing now is a betrayal to this trust and it is a dirty, rotten, treacherous betrayal. Mr. Hughes wants you to know this and here is the message:

"If you ever talk to this girl again, in person or on the telephone, and I know you have her telephone number, or see her or even bump into her on the street (in this case, you should just walk the other way); or if you ever walk or drive anywhere on Coldwater Canyon, or anywhere in that area; or if you are ever seen in the same area where this girl is at any time, you had better get on the first available transportation to Asia, Africa, Europe or South America because if you are in the United States, Canada, Cuba, Mexico, Haiti, the West Indies or Hawaii, I will find you and when I do, you will wish you were dead, and this is not a threat; it is a promise!"

Do you understand that?

It was the first time the hint of violence had been suggested by Hughes or wherever the anonymous message came from. Chouinard delivered it to the man as directed. But he was sure he himself was still going to be fired.

Hughes called with other plans. He ordered Chouinard to fire everyone on his security force. Chouinard was then to continue surveillance on Miss Riverside with a new force made up of Romaine Street Mormons including Mormon Bishop Howard Lundeen. This new system was continued for a few days and then Chouinard called Hughes and said he'd hired entirely new men. The Romaine crew returned to their former duties. Chouinard actually had kept all his old men except for the erring relative who had caused the trouble.

Now Hughes announced the next move. He was moving Miss Riverside from the house to a new residence, a house on Sunset Plaza. But before he did, Hughes explained to Chouinard, he wanted every neighbor within a two-block radius investigated. Chouinard went to work and came back with a detailed report. Everyone looked innocent enough. But the actor Tom Tryon did live about five houses away. Hughes was concerned about this but finally decided to make the move.

Within the rules of the harem pecking-order this move was a definite demotion. Everyone took heart. While The Boss was noncommittal it appeared that at last he was tiring of this strident wench who'd given them all such endless woe for nearly five years.

But no sooner did Hughes give Chouinard official word of the move than another new problem arose. They'd all become increasingly aware in small ways of the Old Man's concern about "the germ thing." But they'd considered it one idiosyncrasy among many. Now he laid out his orders clearly.

Simply stated, although the conversation lasted some forty minutes, Chouinard was ordered to find a cook for the new house who was "neat and clean." She must as well be fine, decent, pure, a religious woman, a nondrinker and nonsmoker, given to going to bed early and getting up early, preferably not too old nor too young nor too fat nor too skinny. She should be paid only a reasonable going wage and her days off would be arranged later.

The next day Chouinard found a middle-aged widow no one had ever met who was a neighbor of a friend in Van Nuys. She was hired immediately. She was a little confused when Chouinard put down the rules Hughes had given him. She must throw away everything she had in her own kitchen—plates, utensils, knives, forks, pots, pans. This was in case she might get one of those promised days off and go home and return to infest Miss Riverside's apartment. Her annoyance ended immediately when Hughes sent a limousine for her to cruise Beverly Hills and pick out new kitchen trimmings and dishes. It was every housewife's dream, like winning one of those "sky's the limit" television quiz shows. She spent several thousand dollars. As for the new house itself, it received a new paint job, new furniture, and a professional shopper refurbished it.

The new locale presented some serious surveillance problems. Roads curved in all directions and there was no way to place a car nearby without being in sight. Further, the men knew they were going to be the focal point of Miss Riverside's wrath. In phone conversations, when she was not cursing Hughes for neglecting her, she was constantly taking out her rage about the men who were spying upon her.

A contractor was building a house a few doors away. Chouinard offered to guard the place free and asked only that he could station a man in it all night. It was nearly finished and the owner was delighted, as vandals in the area were stealing wall fixtures, tropical plants, and the like.

Things went well for the first few weeks. Then one morning the owner called and asked Chouinard to come over to the house. He was irate. "Somebody has had a broad in here," he complained.

"Not one of our men," the detective said bravely but with an inner fear. "It must have been someone else."

He took Chouinard into the living room. On the floor was a broken necklace and there were black footprints all over the lower part of one newly painted wall. The position of the prints made what had been going on obvious.

The culprit had to be one of two men, the ex-marine from Georgia or a college kid, Woody Anderson, the crew concluded. Both denied it. A few days later the ex-marine was fired. Anyone who was efficient enough to say "ten four" didn't belong on the crew anyway. But the contractor was still upset. He threw them out.

The next observation post was a house three doors down, which cost $700 a month. The real estate agent had suggested it because the owners were on vacation for two months. Chouinard's father-in-law and mother-in-law moved in. The house had a closed-circuit television on the roof that scanned the road, and a detective with a two-way radio sat in a car around the corner two blocks away. Then the owners returned from their trip and it was time to move once again.

They had to find a new place and started canvassing the area. There was one dead-end street that curved above and looked down on the house in question. There were five houses on the street, comprising a sort of gay commune. Homosexuals owned the first four houses, a lesbian couple the last. The male gays refused to help when Chouinard explained he was a narcotics officer and wanted to survey a house below. They were fearful of police in any shape.

Chouinard took his wife with him to call on the lesbians, trying to look respectable. He used the same story about being a narcotics officer and asked only that he be able to put one man on their front lawn. They refused. He found out later they thought he was some kind of a pimp with a girl working below and were outraged at the low morals pervading the neighborhood.

Then someone found a homosexual who ran a gift shop, and whose house was ideal. He listened to Chouinard's story and allowed him to use his guest room. By placing a chair on the table the stakeout man could keep a surveillance on the apartment through a high window with binoculars.

It lasted a few days. One Saturday night the host had a party. One of his guests started looking for the bathroom and wandered into the guest room. He found the surveillance man sitting on a chair on the table and went back nervously to the host. "There's a man sitting on a chair on top of a table with binoculars staring out the window. What's going on?"

His host was up to the occasion. "Yeah," he nodded. "He's a friend. He gets his kicks that way. Don't knock it if you haven't tried it."

Sexual liberation was just coming in. The gay guest nodded sympathetically, wondering at the quaint hangups of mankind.

Everyone settled back with the feeling it was just a matter of time before the Old Man dumped Miss Riverside. Then something happened that destroyed all hope. Hughes made an unprecedented move. He bought her a new Chrysler convertible! It was inexplicable, this gift that gave her new freedom and mobility just when everyone felt he was tiring of her. The job was going to be ten times as difficult.

A few days later she took off one sunny afternoon, driving out Sunset Boulevard to the beach. One man tailed her and watched her enter a small shop. She came out with a few packages and returned to the apartment.

The incident was reported to Romaine Street as routine. An hour later there was a call from Hughes. "Jeff, I want your people to go out to that shop and find out exactly what they sell and what kind of customers they have. Call me back tomorrow morning. Then check with the cook and find out what that girl bought." It seemed nonsense, but the next morning Hughes was notified that she'd bought some long matches to light fires in the fireplace, a colorful mitten to pick up hot dishes, and six wineglasses. As for the store, it catered to local householders in the Pacific Palisades area.

The Boss groaned. Chouinard didn't know it then but later realized what the incident meant: The Old Man would have to wait a long time for the germs to die before he visited Miss Riverside again.

As it turned out, he was never to see her again. She was to be the last of the harem.

Her new freedom was more than she could handle. Detectives filed almost daily reports of her misbehavior. She'd stopped at a taco stand and eaten. One afternoon she went to a movie. She'd been seen handling disease-laden paper money. Her years of frustration, loneliness, and isolation were finished. In a sense some of the crew almost felt sorry for her.

One afternoon she was cruising up Hollywood Boulevard when two boys pulled up beside her and gave a wolf whistle. She giggled, stopped, and chatted and then ended up exchanging phone numbers. This report started a new flurry of jitters on Romaine Street. Detectives checked out the license number and put the owner under surveillance.

Romaine Street kept making nervous calls to Chouinard asking if anything new had developed. From phone taps his men knew she was talking to no one except Hughes, but they also had to report she'd been seen making calls from phone booths.

One rainy night she suddenly broke out of the apartment at 11:15 with a sweater held over her head and started running down the hill. A surveillance man gave chase. She ran five blocks and went into a stucco apartment house. Stakeouts waited in the rain through the night. At six in the morning she emerged and walked sedately back up the hill.

The whole Hughes machinery went into high gear. Men started interviewing people in the building she'd visited. Crews were pulled off surveillances of other girls to check everyone in the neighborhood who came and went. Hughes ordered hourly reports on all activities. Romaine Street dropped everything awaiting concrete news of what it was all about.

Hughes had always been fearful of placing girls in neighborhoods where young actors might live. He considered them venomous threats who could cause all kinds of romantic trouble. How she met the man she'd spent the night with no one ever discovered. He was a would-be actor, the stripper Tempest Storm's boyfriend. Miss Storm, it was discovered later, was out of town.

But the real tragedy was yet to come. His name was Sam Rand and he lived on Sunset Plaza about three blocks above Miss Riverside's house. How they met was also never discovered, but he was young, handsome, and dangerous. He moved with a gang of toughs who worked at odd jobs as clerks in liquor stores, as bartenders, or in gas stations but were suspected of peddling marijuana and being part of a burglary ring. Sam himself carried a .45 automatic at times.

The couple was soon giving the vast Hughes organization

daily fits. She'd pick him up while surveillance men tailed them. They'd take off at speeds of eighty miles an hour on the freeways.

"Don't let them get out of sight," Hughes shouted. But the men would lose them. "God damn it!" he'd cry. "We've got all the money in the world. Get twenty cars if you have to! But don't let them get away from you!"

Chouinard tried to explain that this wasn't the problem. Hughes wouldn't listen. "Hire some of those movie stunt drivers if you have to," he ordered.

In the midst of this frantic turmoil Bob Maheu suddenly appeared for the first time. Chouinard found out later Hughes had called him in Washington, D.C., and asked him to come West to help out. Maheu tried to arrange for a deputy sheriff to arrest Sam Rand for carrying a gun. Somehow it didn't come off in time.

More stakeout men were moved to Miss Riverside's house on Hughes' order. Chouinard's top man, Larry Lewis, was stationed at the former residence on Coldwater Canyon in case she came by to pick up some belongings she'd left. He'd been there several days when Rand and Miss Riverside arrived. Rand pulled his .45 and forced Lewis to stand with his face to the wall and with his hands up as Miss Riverside hurriedly packed. They then left to hole up.

Maheu brought a new crew from Washington, D.C., and these men tried to keep tabs on the couple. They failed completely, these former CIA and FBI men. A deal was made with a rental agency for faster cars, although no one could effectively tail Rand, who was like a maniac at the wheel of the convertible.

Then one day Chouinard's detective Bob Roberts stayed on them as they whipped down Sunset Boulevard. They set out for downtown Los Angeles, took a branch freeway, and then Bob lost them at a turnoff.

He called in.

"Keep at it," he was ordered by Chouinard. "Just keep cruising and try to pick them up." There was nothing else to do.

It was early evening when Bob Roberts called back. "I found their car," he said. "It's abandoned at a shooting range. I also found Sam Rand. He's dying in a hospital."

Chouinard was excited. "You're sure you didn't have anything to do with it like running him off the road?" he asked.

"No, of course not. I can't find out what's happened."

"Stay around the hospital until you can find out something," he was ordered.

About midnight Roberts called again. Rand had a critical gunshot wound. The police report said the couple had stopped for some pistol practice. His .45 had jammed and Rand had checked it to see what was the trouble, looking right down the barrel. It had gone off just at that moment.

He died at five that morning. The terrible five long years with Miss Riverside were over.

As for Hughes, it was as if she never existed. He was never even to ask Chouinard what had happened.

CHAPTER 27

SOON AFTER THE CLOSING OF THE MISS RIVERSIDE CASE Bob Maheu casually settled in as part of the hierarchy of the Hughes operation. Old hands, undoubtedly jealous, gossiped that Hughes didn't really trust Maheu and wouldn't give him any serious assignment. At Romaine Street it was claimed that Hughes had given orders that he didn't want to talk to Maheu on the phone.

It was an odd start to a business arrangement, but, then again, it was no more confusing than most of the things The Boss did. Everyone settled back to see what would develop.

Maheu, a French-Canadian from Maine like Chouinard, was about forty-seven at the time. Balding, of medium build and with an engaging personality, people tended to like him immediately. The first night they met, in Long Beach at a beauty-contest fracas, Chouinard and Maheu retired to a hotel room to drink and tell stories of their various security operations. It was clear as Maheu recounted funny spy tales that he wanted Chouinard to expand on what he, a newcomer to the operation, might expect with Hughes. They drank and talked until five. The next morning Maheu was up at eight and hard at work, a sign of the toughness others were to note as time passed.

Maheu wasted no time in establishing his base. He closed his office in Washington, D.C., leased a large house in Brentwood, moved his family out, and took offices in the Kirkeby Building on Wilshire Boulevard. He had soon made a friend of Nadine Henley, Hughes' private secretary of many years. She found Maheu amusing and fun.

Once settled, Maheu had a dinner party for the top Hughes

people in the operations center. One of the non-Romaine guests was Johnny Roselli. It was generally known that Roselli was a top Mafia contact in Las Vegas and a fixer of sorts between the underworld and the outside. He was constantly under surveillance by the FBI and was considered a very tough character. Maheu, a former FBI agent, had reportedly spent much recent time as a CIA operator who did subcontracting work for the agency. Just how Roselli was to be utilized by the Hughes organization and why he'd been invited to meet Bill Gay, Nadine, and others left many puzzled. But it was a merry party. Maheu had a shipment of Maine lobsters flown in and even Bill Gay was happy in his own way.

Years later the Hughes people were to read Roselli's testimony of his involvement with the CIA, the plot to kill Castro, and his complaint that no one ever seemed to consider the patriotic things he'd done all his life. "I even did things for Howard Hughes," he was quoted as saying.

When they found Roselli dead in a barrel in Biscayne Bay in 1976 it was to start a new round of wild tales of Hughes' involvement with the CIA, plots to kill Castro, and gangsters.

CHAPTER 28

By 1960 AN UNEASY PEACE HAD BEEN ESTABLISHED BEtween Howard Hughes, the frenzied girl chaser, and his exhausted staff. The headaches of keeping tabs on women seemed over for the Romaine Street executives and they all felt they could return to more important business. Hughes' disenchantment with Miss Riverside seemed to have cured him. Also, everyone knew his illness was getting worse. "His male menopause or change of life or whatever you call it is over," Chouinard told his wife. Like the others, he was enjoying the calm. For weeks there hadn't been a single surveillance on a girl or any wild expenditures for the once elaborate stable of females. The general theory was that Hughes' fear of germs had at last overcome his sex urge, and he simply wouldn't risk ever again being near a woman.

They should have known better. After a restful interval of some three months all hell broke loose. The furor started at about eleven o'clock one night.

The detective turned on the television to catch the late news and got the Miss Universe Contest at the Lafayette Hotel in Long Beach. He remembers he was taken with Miss Belgium, a beautiful blonde. "Hughes would have gone for her in the old days," he remembers thinking, even though The Boss ordinarily didn't care too much for blondes. Chouinard turned off the set and went to bed.

About an hour later his phone rang. It was Walter Kane, his voice a combination of fear, despair, and urgency. "The Boss wants you to get all of your best men right away and go down to the Long Beach beauty contest. He wants to find out about Miss USA, Miss Belgium, Miss Canada, Miss

France, Miss Switzerland, Miss Austria, and Miss England. He says to get moving right away." The phone went dead.

Chouinard got up and lit a cigarette. He didn't know much about beauty contests but he knew it was futile to go down there in the middle of the night. The girls had chaperones and were surrounded by guards. To hell with it, he thought, and went back to bed.

Early the next morning the phone rang again. It was Kane. Chouinard signaled to his wife, and she said he'd been gone somewhere all night.

Chouinard called Bob Roberts and they set out for Long Beach more as a lark than really to accomplish anything. When they got there they ran into Christy Shepherd, the Hughes photographer, looking bleary-eyed and sleepy. He too had been alerted the previous night and had been waiting in hotel lobbies, wondering what to do, since one in the morning. They called in to Romaine Street to ask for instructions and only then found out what they were involved in. Hughes had been watching the beauty contest in his bungalow last night. All those dormant glands had apparently exploded. He'd first called Kane to alert Christy and Chouinard. Then he'd awakened Maheu and told him to start negotiating to get the girls out of the contest immediately, at any cost. Finally he'd rousted Greg Bautzer, the Beverly Hills lawyer, and told him to get up and start looking for a defunct production company as a cover. To Bautzer's glory, he'd already found and bought a dead firm by that morning, something called the Black Gold Production Company. Under no circumstances was anyone to know Howard Hughes had anything to do with it, they were informed.

Maheu had arrived by now and they all milled helplessly about the lobby of the hotel where the girls were staying. The best they could do was hope to spot some of them. There was nowhere even to start. To comply with Hughes' wishes, they'd have had to close down the show or kidnap the top contestants. Christy was trying his best to find the girls on the list and photograph them according to Hughes' standard orders. As for Chouinard putting his men on duty to tail the girls, it appeared they'd end up in jail even if they could find them.

They spent the day wandering about and answering frantic calls from Romaine Street asking about what progress they were making. Hughes himself, it was obvious, was in an uproar, yelling for more action.

The peace of the past weeks at Romaine Street had now turned into new despair. "If we'd only known the Old Man was watching that show we could have sent a man out to pull the antenna," one staff member quipped.

Slowly, they began to make some progress. They got to know the chaperones and in a few days Christy was getting his photos. By the time the show ended, they'd contacted all the girls and offered screen tests and possible movie contracts with Black Gold Productions. Things were falling into shape. Virginia Tremaine, the Los Angeles real estate woman who handled Hughes' leases, was out searching for suitable apartments and houses. Of twelve, they transported seven contestants and their chaperones to temporary quarters at the Westwood Manor, the Town House, and the Beverly Hills and Beverly Wilshire hotels. Hughes had rejected five girls from the photos. Ordinarily they'd have set it up so none of the girls knew of the others but in this case the contestants had established such camaraderie during the show that trying to isolate them was futile.

Things calmed down a bit, but the Hughes people still imagined hearing the frantic pounding of that Frankenstein monster locked in his Beverly Hills bungalow. They encountered one thorny problem before they got the girls out of Long Beach. An aggressive female theatrical agent from Indiana had been sniffing around and had picked up the smell of greenbacks. She'd been trying to sign up as her clients each of the same girls Black Gold Productions was interested in. Obviously, Hughes' men didn't want any agents involved. They befriended the woman and tried to steer her away, without much success. Chouinard discussed with the other Hughes people the possibility of having to pay her off.

The girls and their chaperones knew little of such things as movie agents, of course. Luckily, the language barrier made it difficult for the anxious agent. Indeed, at one point, as they stood in the lobby, she asked Chouinard, who she'd discovered spoke French, to act as her interpreter with Miss Switzerland on the phone. He started talking to the girl in French and told her exactly the opposite of what the agent had asked. Don't sign anything, Chouinard explained, she just wants to get 15 percent of your money. Stay away from her. He hung up and the agent thanked him profusely for his help.

Christy Shepherd had gone through his bad moments too. When he'd tried to photograph Miss Austria in the conventional way the girl's enthusiastic coach wouldn't leave it at that. "Take off your clothes," she kept ordering the girl.

"No, no, no! She doesn't have to do that," Christy had cried. But the girl had stripped down to the buff while Christy retreated in embarrassment.

A week later things had fallen into place. The girls had dreams of stardom in their eyes, Romaine Street had grudgingly worked up a new girl budget to pay for yet another kookie enterprise, and men were keeping track of the starlets' every move, checking their mail and rooms and filing daily reports on all activities.

Tailing the girls became a complicated chore. They were all tourists in a new city and were out constantly. One day Chouinard and Roberts ran into a problem at the Farmer's Market, a tourist mecca. They were following Miss France and Miss Belgium in the huge crowd and had to stay close. One of the exits was an arcade with a pet shop. As the girls were leaving through this long shop, the detectives some twelve feet behind, a parrot let loose a loud wolf whistle. The girls turned and glared at the men. From then on different detectives had to be assigned to follow them.

After three weeks the girls were becoming more and more restless. There were no screen tests, no contracts, and nothing had happened. At Romaine Street there was grumbling as the costs mounted. From the Beverly Hills Hotel bungalow there was only silence. Everyone was afraid to ask the Old Man what he had in mind. He, in turn, seemed to have forgotten the girls completely after originating his elaborate plan. Slowly, they began to leave for home. First this, then that one. When they talked to people about Hollywood none of them had ever heard of the mysterious Black Gold Production Company.

Chouinard befriended Miss USA, a beautiful and sweet girl from Indiana. She was engaged to a young man, a hometown boy who wanted to become a professional golfer. Chouinard couldn't envision her as one of the Hughes stable and knew she wasn't the type to face the hazards of Hollywood. One day he took her home to meet his wife. The Chouinards pleaded with her to go home and forget the whole thing, explaining the brittle world she'd have to live in. They didn't tell her, however, that she was a Hughes target. The next day she quietly packed and departed.

Hughes was outraged when he got word of this. He emerged from hiding. He called Romaine Street, berating Bill Gay, then turned his wrath on poor Walter Kane, who had nothing to do with any of it. Everyone was blamed but Chouinard, who listened sympathetically as Hughes called him to denounce the other employees.

The Hughes people had been listening to Miss England's phone conversations to her home. She, too, had a boyfriend, was suspicious of the whole vague arrangement, and was homesick. A few days after Miss USA departed, Miss England disappeared and left for home. There was a new round of indignation as the frenzied Mr. Hughes—who had seen none of them except on the television screen and Christy Shepherd's photos—tried to find out what was happening. Again, Bill Gay and Walter Kane took the brunt of the fury. But the infection had spread, and within a week only Miss Belgium was left while Hughes ranted over the phone to his subordinates about their incompetency.

Miss Belgium was a wistfully charming beauty, a Brigitte Bardot with more curves. She could speak no English but was fun-filled and brimming with exuberance. They'd hired a French female coach to teach her English, and this was her only friend. Hughes was determined at any cost to hold on to her. At the Westwood Manor men kept constant vigil and checked her suite every time she left. They were monitoring her phone calls and found she too had a boyfriend back in Belgium. She'd been assigned a car and a driver who could speak French and was constantly on the go seeing the sights and following the busy routine Black Gold had arranged for her "to make you a star." She could be a bit of a tease. One bellhop had a complaint. The first thing she'd do when she arrived back at the suite would be to strip off all her clothes, crawl into bed, and call room service for a drink and food. When he arrived with the tray she'd casually let the cover fall back to give him a brief glimpse of her breasts, then hurriedly pull back in embarrassment. "That broad's crazy," the bellhop grumbled.

The detectives heard of this and, out of boredom as much as anything, decided to amuse themselves. They knew her pattern when she'd return to the hotel was to strip, then pull the venetian blinds shut. One of them went up to her suite when she was gone and jimmied one end of the blinds. That night she came home, stripped, then went over to pull the blinds, which wouldn't work. In the buff, she tugged desperately while five men stood down near the pool giggling like schoolboys.

She still didn't know she was being groomed by Hughes. At least that's what everyone thought until one day one of the Romaine drivers, checking her wastebasket when she was out, found a letter from Belgium written in French and torn into small bits. He thought it might be a letter from her boyfriend. Chouinard went to work to find out. It took hours to glue the bits together and then to translate the letter. It was from her mother, and somehow in distant Belgium the mother had found out Howard Hughes was behind the whole affair. She was in a panic, having read of his exploits, and ordered her daughter to come home. But Hughes' people were desperate to keep this last girl from getting away. The Old Man was haranguing them daily and denouncing them for allowing the others to leave. But the wiretappers knew from her phone calls that she was determined to be back in Belgium for Christmas. It was only a few weeks away.

The Hughes men told her she couldn't leave, that if she skipped out she could never work in movies, in Europe or anywhere else again. Meanwhile, she had only the lady who was her coach to talk with, who was, after all was said and done, another Hughes spy.

One day she sneaked away and got to the Belgian Consul and pleaded with him to get her out of the country. Hughes' people had tailed her, however, and Romaine Street operatives followed up and somehow killed any effort to help her. She had to stay.

By now the attempt to keep this lone girl a prisoner was absorbing most of the efforts of a dozen people, who held solemn meetings plotting new ways not to let her get away. Kay Glenn, who had escorted her everywhere because Hughes trusted him above everyone, grumbled that he'd hoped to get back to Utah for Christmas but he was sure the Old Man wouldn't let him go as long as Miss Belgium was around. He was an ardent family man and terribly annoyed. Chouinard made a five-dollar bet that he'd be able to go.

Chouinard began to call the girl and talk with her in French. Just to have someone to chat with was a delight for her and she seemed to develop almost a romance with her mystery caller. About then Hughes decided to shift her and moved the girl and the coach into an apartment in Westwood. It gave Chouinard an opportunity to call Bill Gay. "It's getting harder and harder to tail this girl," he explained. "She's suspicious and mad. She keeps dodging us and getting away. Why don't I simply start driving her myself so I'll have some control."

Gay was frantic, taking daily tongue-lashings from Hughes about his incompetence in letting the other girls get away. He agreed quickly. As soon as Chouinard started driving her she realized that he was the mystery caller. He told her in French that really all she had to do was leave. It was a free country despite her impressions and no one could hold her even if they'd intimidated her into believing she was their prisoner.

The day came when she packed and was ready to leave for the airport. Chouinard had convinced her to do it but had to protect himself. He called Romaine Street to report what she was doing.

He drove her to the airport. By the time they got there she was being paged on the phone. Greg Bautzer was calling. It was a last-ditch effort to stop her, and he was apparently telling her all the awful things that could happen to her and her career if she left. She started to cry as Chouinard watched her at the phone, but he hustled her toward the exit for the plane. "Don't be afraid, nothing can happen," he kept telling her. Just as he was saying it, however, he saw a police helicopter start to land next to the plane. Good God, he thought, this is going too far; this is the limit, if they've arranged to grab her just as she is boarding the plane. Chouinard was outraged and thought to himself, "To hell with this. If they try to grab her, I'm going to blow the whistle on everything."

But it seemed they were on some other business, and she went aboard and, moments later, took off for home.

The whole fiasco had a final irony to it, making Hughes the victim once again. For she married the actor Stewart Granger in Europe some time later, the man Chouinard had tailed to Africa when Hughes was trying to woo Jean Simmons, his wife. Hughes had not only failed to do that but Granger had ended up with Hughes' potential mistress as his wife. As far as Chouinard knows, Hughes never actually even met Miss Belgium, the girl who created such chaos for the whole operation. She died young.

Bill Gay was the major victim. Hughes was so outraged at the way all his seven beauty queens had escaped that he didn't speak to Gay for a year. He denounced Gay viciously the day Miss Belgium departed and ordered him to pack up and leave. "Go home. I never want to see you again," he ordered. Gay retreated to his home in Encino and set up an office in the house. He stayed on the payroll and Hughes eventually started speaking to him again. But Gay seldom went back to Romaine Street. Later he opened an office near his home, which he occupies today while Romaine Street remains more or less a front.

Mean and desperate as his chores have been, Chouinard likes to think that during this episode he saved two nice girls from—as the old saying goes—a fate worse than death.

CHAPTER 29

THIS DILEMMA OF FINDING WAYS TO COPE WITH THE OLD Man's driving desire to deal with ladies in quantity often led to some outlandish escapades. One of the wilder confusions came just before noon on a New Year's Eve when Chouinard was called to report to Romaine on a secretive matter of great urgency. When he arrived, he found a grim-faced Bill Gay and a worried Kay Glenn sitting silently.

"We've got a real problem and it's going to take some doing to pull it off," Bill Gay explained. Chouinard sat stunned as the plot unfolded. While it was not as momentous as the TWA crisis, it seemed to be as serious to the Mormons. Simply stated, Howard Hughes had decided he wanted to have New Year's dinner at midnight at the Beverly Hills Hotel with three women—none of whom were to be aware of the presence of the other two!

As the discussions went on, it was obvious the Old Man had already given his finest attention to the logistics of the plot and been working it out in detail for some time. For it was all intricately laid out, involving a dozen people who had to follow the timing of the choreography down to the second.

Jean Peters was to be in the dining room of the hotel, Susan Hayward was to be at a table in the Polo Lounge, and his Number 3, a would-be starlet, "the Coldwater Party," was to be in a back bungalow at a candlelit table. At a few minutes before the magic hour Hughes would be with Jean Peters in the dining room. They would order cocktails and the Old Man would be interrupted by a phone call. Complaining about the press of business, he'd excuse himself and hurry to the

Polo Lounge, where Susan Hayward would be waiting, having been brought to the hotel with perfect timing by a chauffeur. He'd order drinks and again an aide would interrupt with a business phone call. He'd excuse himself and hurry back to the bungalow to settle down briefly with "the Coldwater Party," only to be called away again.

As it was orchestrated, each girl would dine in a hit-and-miss style with Hughes with three interruptions each while the Old Man complained of the pressures of a big deal pending. The maître d's in both the Polo Lounge and dining room were part of the game plan and would alert various sentinels if anything went astray. Chouinard's mission was a pleasant and simple one. He was stationed outside the bungalow in the rear. If "the Party" got testy—as she had a tendency to do—and tried to bolt, he was to alert Kay Glenn, in the lobby, who would head her off. Part of Chouinard's job, as usual, was not to be seen.

It started well enough. Hughes sat down to shrimp cocktails with each in turn and scurried on to the next course. The merry sounds of horns and bells were heard at midnight as Chouinard sat outside completely disgruntled.

Then, because of a female's sixth sense, all hell broke out at once. As Hughes made his apologetic departure from Miss Hayward and the Polo Lounge for the second time to answer a phone call, she apparently became suspicious, and under the pretext to the maître d' of having to powder her nose, tailed him into the dining room. "The Party," who'd been left alone in the bungalow too long, started angrily up the walk to the hotel. Frantically, Chouinard called Kay Glenn, who had been diverted by the Hayward maneuver.

Susan had by then cornered Hughes with Jean Peters. He sat flushed and embarrassed while the redheaded actress loudly denounced him with Brooklyn adjectives and stormed out in a rage. Jean Peters, vaguely aware of what was going on, got up and left just as the indignant "Party" attacked the lobby to fire another volley of curses at the Old Man and was intercepted by Kay. Hughes got up, a lonely, lank, and tired man, and walked away.

But he recovered quickly. Within an hour he was calling Romaine and various assistants, trying to find people to denounce. For three days he hurled accusations at different members of the staff for fouling up his elaborate scheme. Fortunately, Chouinard's task had been an easy one and he'd done it, so Hughes couldn't blame him.

Susan Hayward never saw Hughes again as far as anyone knows. Back in 1955 the Old Man had timed things better with the fiery, red-haired actress. She'd attempted suicide, which had upset Hughes. He'd called Chouinard when he found out that she was returning home from the hospital. "I've ordered a big bunch of roses. I want you to be waiting for her when she arrives at home. Be standing on the steps and don't be one minute late. Hand them to her personally just as she gets to the door. Say they're from me."

That had worked out. It was simpler.

CHAPTER

30

IN THE EARLY 1960'S CHOUINARD WAS TO FIND HIMSELF IN a terrible jam as a result of his endless efforts to recruit new detectives.

A neighbor, Stan Atkinson, who was a newscaster, brought in a well-dressed and clean-cut man in his midthirties who claimed he desperately wanted to work for Hughes. His credentials were impeccable. He was an administrative assistant to a Congressman from Glendale and had been active in the Rockefeller campaign. Yet something didn't ring true. Why, Chouinard wondered, would a fellow with his background want to stand guard duty at some empty house or sit in a surveillance car for days? Chouinard took him to his house for a drink, and his wife was equally suspicious as was Betty O'Dell, an employee of his.

But Atkinson swore by the young man. The newscaster had covered Sacramento, the state capital, as a reporter, and he knew him well, he claimed. Chouinard decided to try him as a salesman rather than a guard. He had some cards printed with his name on them and sent him out to try to find outside business for the Mike Conrad Agency. While he'd never directly asked the Old Man whether he could have outside accounts, it was a period with nothing happening and he felt he could keep his men working if he could find a few other things to do. This newcomer was the picture of a wholesome, Republican go-getter and would be ideal, he concluded.

No sooner had he hired him and given him the car than the man asked about a gun permit.

"We don't carry guns," Chouinard explained, "and you certainly don't need one to sell accounts." Chouinard went on to lecture him, concerned that he was some kind of freak even to ask. "I've found my men with guns in the glove compartments on stakeouts and fired them on the spot," he warned. "None of us ever carry firearms. Is that understood?" The man was all apologies but Chouinard told him to wait a day or so before he put him on the payroll.

The man never actually was to work for him. He disappeared and didn't report back for work. Chouinard forgot about him.

Then he received a call from Romaine. He was informed that Maheu had told Romaine that the FBI was looking for Chouinard. In fact, they'd been looking for Chouinard for some weeks, Maheu said, and had hit a dead end but then had heard Chouinard was somehow involved with Hughes.

Inadvertently, Chouinard had covered his tracks well. There was no detective agency under the name of Jeff Chouinard, the name Stan Atkinson had used to introduce him to the applicant, and the FBI could make no connection. In keeping with the Old Man's advice, Chouinard's house was under still another name and his utilities were paid under the name of George Nelson.

He was later to find out through Romaine what it was all about. The well-groomed youth who had applied for a job was in love with an opera singer and had been buying her fur coats, diamonds, and stereo equipment. He was leading a double life. He was rooming with a fellow who was a lobbyist for the California Medical Association. He'd come home several times a week, taking great rolls of bills from his pockets. "I'm working for a guy who is a private detective for Howard Hughes," he explained to his roomie, "and they pay me off in cash." He'd shown one of his cards.

He was holding up banks. He'd tried to go to work for Chouinard simply to get a legal gun permit.

The FBI had traced Chouinard by contacting the former Hughes detective he'd replaced, who was only too glad to blow the whistle on him. "I wouldn't be a bit surprised if that damned Jeff is in on it," he'd told them. "He's a dirty son of a bitch and would do something like that."

Almost immediately the FBI contacted Bob Maheu who, as a former FBI agent, listened to the tale. He said later he wasn't too sure about Chouinard either. After all, he'd just built a $100,000 beach house. Maheu suggested to Chouinard that he call the FBI and talk to them. He did. "Meet me at the security guard's office at the Bel Air gates," he said. They were there within an hour.

"I want to clear this up and nail this guy," Chouinard explained. "I had nothing to do with it." He recounted the episode of his encounter with the bank robber and they seemed to believe him.

The criminal had hit only a few days before, robbing a Western Union office. Twelve different bank tellers had identified him from photos from previous jobs. Shortly after Chouinard's meeting with the FBI they caught the man and he identified two accomplices who'd run for Miami. Both had been arrested as homosexuals in the past. Their photos went on wanted bulletins and a month or so later one of them called the FBI office in Miami. "We understand you want us," he said, giving his name. "We want to give ourselves up."

The agent on phone duty said, "Report here as soon as you can."

"We'll be there in half an hour," the voice replied. They didn't show. A few days later their bodies were found in their car on Biscayne Boulevard. They'd apparently made a suicide pact.

As for the handsome dude, he later got eighty-eight years for eleven different bank robberies, and Chouinard resolved to be more careful in giving out ID cards.

Chouinard lived in this gray world of shifting identities for some years at the Old Man's instruction. His neighbors didn't know what he did. He'd learned the need to keep that secret early when he'd moved into North Hollywood and found himself next to a very quiet and elderly couple. They were soon curious about the continual calls he got. Men on duty called day and night to report in, the Old Man called with a number of demands each day. All night they'd hear ringing because he'd often forget to disconnect a phone he had near the pool that was next to their bedroom window.

They couldn't stand it much longer and asked their daughter —the Chouinards' baby-sitter—about it. Chouinard couldn't come up with anything but the truth, that he was a private detective.

Even his own son of six was silent about his activities. At one point Chouinard arranged to go to Palm Springs to live for a few months during the winter despite Hughes' complaints that it would foul up operations. As it turned out Chouinard wasn't missed because Hughes was constantly on his back and he spent most of his time in Los Angeles. But during the brief respite, Perry Lieber, one of Hughes' top aides, called Chouinard and asked him as a friend to cover an assignment at Palm Springs. Mervyn LeRoy's daughter had separated from David May, scion of the department-store family, who was in Los Angeles, and there was some fear May might create a scene. Perry asked Chouinard to stay with her for a time in the evenings when she was alone. Once the detective took his son along and on the way over explained what they were going to do and tried to give him an idea of what his job was.

The child sighed with relief as if he'd been carrying a deep worry for a long time. "Gee, Dad, that's great! You know I thought you was a robber!" The boy had grown up listening to Chouinard on the phone with such gangster television jargon as "put one man on the corner and another on stakeout and when the car drives up let me know . . ."

Chouinard used a variety of aliases when he was on a Hughes assignment at an out-of-town hotel. Usually he posed as a playboy who had money. If he was pressed to explain his business, he sometimes said he had a crop-dusting firm in California's San Joaquin Valley. He doesn't know why he selected this offbeat business except that he'd done some of it years before and very few people are familiar with it.

It caused a serious problem for him at Roy Evans' Racquet Club in Florida at one time. Some chums he'd met at the bar decided they'd do him a favor. They brought over an outgoing and corpulent man in a bright jacket. They introduced him, explaining that he was "the Cucumber King of Florida."

He lit a cigar and started quizzing Chouinard about his rates, how many planes he had, and when he was available. Chouinard went into a long harangue about moving his operation from one coast to the other and convinced him he'd be too expensive. Chouinard was anxious to change the subject.

As he shifted from hotel to hotel at the Old Man's bidding, posing as a playboy bachelor, he made up new aliases as he went, calling in regularly to inform Romaine of his newest name. This often led to trouble. He'd introduce himself carefully at poolside or the tennis court with his newest name and then forget. The loudspeaker would start paging him and he wouldn't respond while his new companions would look at him curiously.

Such a scene occurred at the Bombay Hotel in Miami, where he was living in his role as a bachelor. One day he was paged and, as often, had to be told to respond. There was a telegram at the desk for him. Because of its nature and because they all knew him, it had been read and discussed by everyone at the desk before they handed it to him. It was from his wife in Burbank.

"Today our little baby died. Cancer of the pancreas and it will be buried tomorrow."

He carried on as if nothing had happened.

That night one of his newfound pals came up to express his sorrow. "But you're the lousiest bastard I ever knew," he added. Chouinard had to go around explaining to everyone that "Baby" was a thirteen-year-old cocker spaniel.

He'd return from such trips always wary about submitting expense accounts. The routine was simplicity itself: to list one's expenditures, and submit the items and the total to Romaine. He'd heard all the expense-account stories from friends with large corporations. But dealing with Hughes was something different. For you never knew if he had someone following you, carefully chronicling your daily actions. One became paranoid out of one's own knowledge of the Old Man's ways and always wondered if the casual-looking fellow next to you at the table or bar might not just be a spy out to watch you while—just maybe—someone was watching *him.*

This atmosphere of suspicion left all employees tense in any situation involving expenses. Quite likely Hughes might attack on the basis that you'd poor-boyed a certain task and that was why you'd failed. But he was just as likely to question you—always by indirect implication—and infer that you'd spent so much of his money cavorting about that you didn't have time to do the job.

CHAPTER 31

HUGH MACKENZIE, ONCE AN RKO PRESS AGENT, RECALLS sponsoring a beauty contest in Ohio, soon after World War II. The winner was a fetching beauty named Jean Peters. She was sent off to Hollywood and possible stardom.

Hughes once told a crony how he met her. There'd been a large party at his house. When it broke up he had said good-bye to the last guest at the door when he noticed a girl sitting despondently on his front steps. She'd somehow become separated from her friends at the party and was wondering how to get home. He took her back inside and she went to sleep on the couch.

By 1947 she was a serious part of his life. Hollywood gossip items told of the two dining here or attending a party there. Then Hughes got word of a subpoena being issued for him to appear before a Senate committee in Washington, D.C. He had other reasons not to want to face such turmoil besides the obvious disdain he had for public appearances. He decided to cut and run until the political excitement was over. Fearful that he'd be tracked down in any of his usual haunts, he called the private detective Chouinard was later to replace. Hughes ordered the detective to send his family away and explained that he, Hughes, was moving into the detective's house. A small tract home in the San Fernando Valley, it would be the last place a subpoena server would be likely to look, Hughes had concluded.

The detective sent his wife and children to visit her family in Michigan and moved into a hotel. Hughes, Jean Peters, and Hughes' cook moved into the house.

It was all very proper. Hughes took a back bedroom and

Jean the front guest room. Hughes gave her strict orders not even to go into the back yard, as he was convinced anyone who recognized her could lead a subpoena bounty-hunter to his lair.

The detective visited regularly and told Chouinard later how solicitous the Old Man was of Jean's welfare. "He'd go to her door and knock every hour or so, inquiring how she was getting along," the detective explained. "He seemed more concerned about her than he did about the case in Washington."

Eventually he gave himself up and appeared before the committee to face down Senator Brewster, who tried to browbeat him. It was generally felt that Hughes won out in the stormy committee hearings.

Later, Jean was to appear in her first big movie, *Captain from Castille,* which was being made on location in Mexico. Hughes sent along a companion for Jean who was to report the actress's every off-hour activity to Hughes and, if there was any trouble, she was ordered to call him immediately. It was to be the modus operandi during Jean Peters' entire acting career.

Her next part was in *Viva Zapata,* which was also made on location in Mexico. Hughes called Chouinard. "Jeff, I want to ask a big favor of you," he began. The detective was familiar by then with the implications of such an opening. It was a command in disguise and meant there was no way to escape. The Old Man went on to detail the "favor." He wanted Chouinard's wife at the time, Betty Lou, to accompany Jean and stay with her at all times.

Hughes had more than his usual trepidation over this picture for it starred Marlon Brando, who he'd heard was a devil with the ladies. "I want you to watch this Brando fellow and tell me exactly what he does," he instructed Betty Lou when she'd agreed to go along. "I've heard some strange things about him." What Hughes was referring to was simply the publicity buildup that touted Brando as the idol of all women throughout the world.

Betty Lou was vigilant and after a week was able to forward an intelligence report to Chouinard to give to The Boss. "Tell Mr. Hughes not to worry about Brando. He has the sweet mind of a four-year-old and has no interest in chasing women. No spark at all. . . ."

Betty Lou was to accompany Jean when she made *Niagara* with Joseph Cotten. Some of the cast were having dinner together in the hotel dining room when a drunk appeared, carrying a jockstrap, and came over to Marilyn Monroe, who was at the table. He asked her to autograph it. Giggling, Monroe asked for a pen.

Cotten was outraged. "For God's sake, man, go away," he said.

Marilyn was puzzled. "What's wrong?" she asked. "I don't understand." She autographed it while others at the table left.

Apache with Burt Lancaster was to present still a new problem. It was being shot in the High Sierra and Jean, during one of Hughes' daily calls, mentioned casually how cold it was. Hughes immediately chartered a plane and had a pilot fly up a stack of electric blankets.

Hughes' efforts to be helpful sometimes took quaint turns. Chouinard remembers when Betty Lou and Jean were scheduled to fly to a location. They'd picked Jean up at her house on San Ysidro Drive and gone on to the Beverly Hills Hotel to see Hughes and say good-bye. He came limping out toward the auto, wearing one shoe and carrying one in his hand.

"What's wrong, honey?" Jean inquired.

He shook his head sadly like a little boy. "I lost the key to my bungalow and tried to crawl through the window. It slammed down and I cut my foot and now I can't get my shoe on."

Despite this, or maybe because of it, he insisted on driving them to the airport, a most unusual volunteer service for him. No one was happy about it. He was a horrendous driver. He didn't seem to pay attention to what he was doing while he drove at breakneck speed, one shoe off and one shoe on.

It seemed apparent to everyone but Hughes that his jealousy was plain nonsense. Jean Peters was a straightforward, no-nonsense girl from the Midwest. She was easygoing and showed no interest in flirting with anyone. Parties and night life clearly bored her and her favorite recreation was to sit in her room after work with a crossword puzzle. Betty Lou always returned from location feeling she'd served no purpose.

But the Old Man was obviously pleased with her work. When the time came for Jean to go to Rome to make *Three Coins in the Fountain,* Betty Lou was with her once again. She was able to report one incident of minor significance. A group of the cast was lounging in a hotel room having cocktails after the day's work, and Jean was curled up on a bed. One actor reached over and ran his hand along her leg. Jean picked up a portable radio on the nightstand and threw it at him. She missed but it bounced through the open door and clattered down the steps while anxious Italians peered out of doorways wondering what had happened.

Hughes called her every night in Rome, usually with nothing more than inquiries about her day's work, and small talk. Once he called in a rage. *Newsweek* had run an article on his activities. "Go down to the lobby and see if it's on the stand," he instructed her. He told her the page. "Just read it there and put it back on the rack," he went on. "Don't buy it. I don't want those sons of bitches to make any money out of me."

His vigilance was never-ending. It was a joke to others. But perhaps Hughes' concern was eventually justified. When in Rome, Betty Lou had casually reported that a nice man,

Stan Hough, a studio executive with Twentieth Century-Fox, often joined Jean and the rest of the group for dinner. Hughes was immediately on the alert. He called for a complete investigation at once. It showed only that Hough was a married man of fine character. Years later Jean was to marry him.

A more immediate cause for Hughes' jealousy was about to surface.

Jean and Betty Lou had started back to the U.S. from Rome in a half-empty plane. To be more comfortable, each had stretched out on two seats. A fellow passenger, one Stuart Cramer, took a seat across the aisle from Jean and began to chat. He was with the State Department, personable and attractive. By the time the plane landed they were friends. More than that, his timing couldn't have been better.

Jean had apparently been insisting that Hughes marry her. He had, as always, procrastinated. "I don't know why I don't marry this girl," he told Walter Kane at one point. "She's the only girl who has ever really loved me and I'm crazy about her. We have a lot in common—like getting up in the middle of the night for a snack—but I don't know. . . ."

Cramer was not easily put off. After that trip he started visiting Jean, who lived in a small house above Sunset Boulevard and seemed to welcome his visits. Hughes was beside himself. He called Chouinard in. "I want you to put full surveillance on Jean's house," he said. "There's a place across the street that has an embankment with heavy bushes. If you get up there, you can look right into the living room."

As so often happened, Hughes had obviously already visited the area, picked out the spots for surveillance, and knew just what move to make. A man was stationed in the brush but found nothing to report.

Jean's surveillance by Betty Lou had been fine at first, and both had no complaints. But Jean's attitude changed as she felt more and more the pressure of Hughes' jealousy. Then, at the studio, Betty Lou was dubbed "Jean's spy," which galled her. Things became more tense.

Chouinard was in the middle. Betty Lou didn't want to make more trips under such conditions. The Old Man would call. "Look, Jeff, this is a real favor, and I know you have to batch it and what a pain in the ass that is." He'd then launch into another plea for Betty Lou to go on location with Jean just once more. "Jean is anxious to have her along," he'd say. Chouinard knew that was not true. He wasn't getting along with his wife by that time and it didn't concern him at all for her to go away. But it was apparent that Hughes, not Jean, wanted her on the trip.

Chouinard reneged at the last moment a few times. "Betty Lou just doesn't want to go unless Jean wants her," he'd explained. "It puts her in an uncomfortable position."

"No, no, Jeff!" The Boss insisted. "You just don't understand. Jean wants her along."

Chouinard once drove Betty Lou to the airport to find Hughes and Jean arguing, Jean making it clear that she didn't want Betty Lou along. Hughes was furious, but Jean took off alone. That didn't settle it. The next day Hughes was on the phone again. "I talked to Jean last night," he claimed. "She called to say she'd changed her mind and wants Betty Lou to meet her in Europe." They both knew it wasn't true and Betty Lou tried to squirm out. Hughes wouldn't allow it.

"Do you have any cash?" he asked Chouinard after concluding arrangements for Betty Lou to fly out immediately.

"Not enough cash to send her to Europe."

"Call Romaine Street and they'll have some cash ready," he went on. "It will all be taken care of. The ticket is all paid for and at the airport."

Chouinard called Romaine to pick up the cash. "We can't get it that fast," he was informed. "Go on to the airport and we'll have someone meet you."

No one arrived as takeoff time approached. Chouinard called Romaine. "There's a foulup," he was told. "Tell her a man will meet her in Las Vegas."

She got aboard. "Are you going to Paris?" the stewardess asked.

"I'm not sure. Las Vegas or New York or Paris," Betty Lou replied uncertainly.

Chouinard waved good-bye. She called soon after from Las Vegas. No one had met her. She had five dollars. Chouinard called Romaine Street. "Tell her to go on to New York. A man will meet her there with the cash."

Chouinard was indignant. "If there's no one there, she's going to turn around and come back," he threatened. "And I'm going to tell the Old Man why."

"There will be," he was told. "We promise." There was, and Betty Lou made it on to Paris, where a reluctant Jean greeted her once again.

Jean at last forced Hughes to allow her to go alone to locations when she was in a movie. But he'd fret constantly. One day he called Chouinard when she was in Georgia at Stone Mountain making *A Man Called Peter.*

"I want you to get back and see what's going on," he said. "Just stay close. If anything happens, let me know. Don't let her know you're there."

Chouinard took off and, wearing dark glasses, edged through the crowd on location for several days. Knowing Jean's feelings about being secretly spied on, he wished he could approach her and tell her he was there. But he knew he couldn't.

He thought his ruse was working splendidly until one morning the still-man was shooting a group picture of the cast and crew. The detective was standing fifty yards away, hidden in a mob of onlookers, when he heard her yell, "Hey, Jeff, come on and get in the picture!" Chouinard was to find out later the Old Man had told her that the detective would be around if she needed him but then, for secret reasons of his own, as usual, had failed to tell Chouinard that Jean knew he was going to be there.

She never mentioned it again, but she'd sometimes look at him when he was talking about some case involving surveillance and giggle knowingly.

The news of Jean's marriage came as a shock wave to Romaine. There were tales of this Cramer fellow who'd been seen escorting her around town. There were other rumors of the Old Man's fury. Gossip even held that Hughes was backed into a corner and was actually going to marry Jean. The secret courtship of Cramer and Peters had been more or less dismissed as just another eddy in the swirling black waters of Hughes' life.

When news stories broke of the elopement with Cramer the Romaine forces sat back expecting the worst—certainly accusations and blame, maybe mass dismissals. Strangely, there was only silence. No one was called by The Boss to discuss some elaborate plot to discredit Cramer. In a way the ominous quiet was worse than the usual explosion.

Several months later Chouinard got a call from Hughes, who was in Miami. "Come back here right away and register at the Columbus Hotel," The Boss said. "I've got something that has to be handled with absolute secrecy."

A day later the detective flew to Miami, registered, and called Hughes. There was a tone of embarrassment as Hughes chatted about trivia. Then he came to the issue at hand.

"Jean is here in Miami," he began. "She says she doesn't love her husband and wants to divorce him. I'm supposed to help her out. But now you have to try to understand this. I'm supposed to help him, too. I don't know why, but he keeps calling me like I'm his uncle or best friend or something. He wants me to try to get them back together. She wants me to help her keep him away. It's a terrible mixup."

Hughes went on to explain to Chouinard that Jean had hidden herself away in a little house on an island in Biscayne Bay.

"I've given this a lot of thought," Hughes went on, "and this is what I want you to do. I've told Cramer he could talk with Jean tomorrow. Then I told her she had to talk with him. But she's very upset and doesn't want to see him. I finally got her to agree to meet with him alone and I promised I wouldn't be around. I've decided they should meet on a boat. I want you to go charter a fishing boat where they can talk privately. But I want to know what goes on. Arrange for the boat and then get someone who can act like a deckhand who can listen to what's said. I want a full report, everything that's said, every little movement, if they touch hands, if she acts angry with him, if they argue . . . everything."

Chouinard arranged for the boat and then found an airline-ticket salesman who seemed bright and alert. "I'll pay you a hundred dollars and you'll get a free fishing trip," he explained after outlining the duties. The youth was delighted to play detective.

His detailed report later that day wasn't much. The couple had argued about a variety of petty matters for several hours and that was all. Nothing had been resolved.

Hughes now began to stall Cramer, who was calling him to try to find out where Jean was staying. "Jean's pretty upset," Hughes explained. "You are just going to have to let her calm down a bit." Each day when Cramer called, Hughes would cajole him into waiting and staying calm. It was his old tactic of delay and more delay. He was all sympathy as he listened but always suggested Cramer wait just a bit. This went on for eight days. At last Hughes said he'd try to get Jean to agree to meet with Cramer at her place. The meeting was set up for the next evening.

Hughes called Chouinard again. "I want you to go out there and watch through the window and report everything," he ordered. He went on as usual to give the detective a detailed description of the house, the terrain, and the problems he might encounter.

The house faced a canal where dozens of small boats were docked and had a steep lawn running up from the water's edge. There was a large picture window in the living room. After it was dark the detective tiptoed up the incline to peer into the living room. But fate beyond even Hughes' careful planning ended the operation abruptly. The automatic sprinklers went on. Chouinard slid to the water's edge, climbed into a rowboat, and stared unhappily up at the blanket of spray that cut off all view.

Now an uneasy peace set in. Cramer and Jean began seeing each other every day. Hughes was both confused and concerned and called Chouinard several times daily to get his interpretation of what might be happening. Chouinard had none. All he could do was follow the couple at a discreet distance so Jean would not recognize him.

One day they took off for the racetrack, Chouinard in pursuit. At the track he decided he'd better call Hughes to inform him of what was going on. He asked for a pay phone. "Are you wacky?" he was asked. "There aren't any pay phones at racetracks."

The sleuth, who'd never been to a track before, couldn't understand why. But he decided to reach Hughes by telegraphing Romaine, which could then contact the Old Man. He scribbled out his message. "The Party and her escort are at Hialeah. Inform The Boss." The clerk looked at Chouinard with dismay.

"You think you're at Hialeah?" he asked. Chouinard nodded.

"This is Tropical Park."

Chouinard smiled weakly. "Well, change it then," he replied. The only racetrack he'd ever heard of in Miami was Hialeah.

It didn't matter. The next day Jean Peters packed abruptly and flew off to Los Angeles. It seemed the reconciliation had failed beautifully.

Hughes left a day later and Cramer followed soon after. Then there was a new development that confused everyone. Cramer and Hughes became pals. Kay Glenn started taking Cramer golfing. Hughes acted as a busy social secretary, arranging dinner invitations for Cramer to meet new and interesting companions. Then Hughes arranged for a job for him at Lockheed as a junior executive. As a final ironic touch Cramer was eventually to marry Hughes' old girlfriend Terry Moore.

In time, Jean's divorce came. Then Hughes and Jean quietly went to Hawthorne, Nevada, and were married.

They were to live at both the Beverly Hills Hotel and the leased house at Santa Fe for a time. Then, as the darkness of the germ phobia grew increasingly intense, the time came that the Old Man decided to go into hiding in the leased château in Bel Air. It was the beginning of the end. But it was still more than a decade away.

CHAPTER 32

HUGHES WAS TO LIVE IN THE BEL AIR CHÂTEAU FOR SOME seven years. During that time he was never to leave his one bedroom until the day came that his toilet plugged up. It was a fateful decision, and for hours Hughes sat slumped in a chair as the need to defecate grew and grew. He couldn't call in a plumber for fear of the room becoming contaminated. At last he wrapped a towel around his waist and shuffled across the hall to Jean Peters' bathroom. He used it for several days until his own toilet had somehow been repaired and a variety of disinfecting methods employed to cleanse the bathroom of germs.

Jean had been the first to arrive at the château. Chouinard already had guards on full-time duty on the grounds and at the gate. She moved in without fanfare as they stood by, assuming the Old Man would soon follow. Days passed. Detectives knew they'd been living in a leased house at Rancho Santa Fe, an exclusive community of lavish homes north of San Diego. They'd heard also of some of the trouble there. The house had become conspicuous and a subject of local controversy and indignation because Hughes had refused to permit a gardener to come onto the grounds for fear of infection.

The house had been beautifully landscaped. Now the plants had simply dried up and died. Romaine had to replace the plants when Hughes moved, and it cost $50,000.

Jean Peters had passed word on that she didn't want guards near the Bel Air house. She wanted them to stay outside the fence and park on the street. They assumed that this was the Old Man's edict, as she'd shown little concern for such security matters before.

More than a week passed and then word came to pull the men off guard duty at the front gate between five and seven one evening. The guard was to return at seven, however, and the normal security routine was to start again. It was an obvious announcement that Hughes was due to arrive. Chouinard did as directed, then went to the gate and pulled the guard aside. They hid in the bushes near the entrance to see if the stories they'd heard of Hughes' condition were true.

Shortly after six a black Cadillac limousine drove slowly up to the gate. Two men no one had seen before were in the front seat. One got out and opened the gate. The driver pulled through and the gate was closed behind the auto. On the floor of the back seat, covered with a black blanket, was a big bundle. Howard Hughes had arrived.

A routine was quickly established. At first various Hughes executives came and went. Food started arriving three times a day from the Beverly Hills Hotel. Old drivers who had worked for Hughes years before reappeared, working eight-hour shifts inside the house. It was interesting to note that these men weren't all Mormons. Holmes was a Catholic, Harris and Crawford were Presbyterians. Such religious affiliations would have meant little in most circumstances, but this made it clear that Hughes had selected men other than Mormons for fear he might be dominated by the clique. An old-timer in the Hughes operations could read the Old Man's strategy as clearly as a road sign. Moreover, it was clear he wasn't as mad as rumored.

All this time no one was officially told that Hughes was inside, but gossip and idle conversation among the personnel soon established that the Old Man was in a certain room, that the old drivers were serving him as aides, sitting on the toilet in the bathroom awaiting his summons. Hughes himself had ordered all windows sealed with masking tape and installed a red warning light above the interior door. When it was lit it meant that no one was to enter. It was always lit.

The room was barren, with heavy drapes always pulled tight

against the sunlight, a bed, a straight-backed chair, telephones, two nightstands, and a television set. The nightstands were piled high with directives, business papers, and memos, which were brought in each day and stacked, but seldom were given attention by Hughes. Rather, he sat for hours in the chair, naked, with a towel over his lap, watching old films. He ate, as usual, steak, salad, tomato juice, and Poland water. This was the setting people pieced together from the conversations of the old drivers as they went in and out.

Hughes was listless and silent most of the time but would now and again erupt into a fury of activity, making dozens of phone calls, reading, ruffling through the stacks of memos and scribbling replies on yellow legal-size tablets, then reverting to apathy again for days on end. He slept by his own time clock, usually for four hours at a time after reaching exhaustion. As he seemed to enjoy most of the hoary old movies that run on Los Angeles television between midnight and dawn his hours were often adjusted to their appearance.

At times he turned into a psychotic tyrant. One aide, Roy Crawford, a mild-mannered if not timid man, had done a ten-hour stint sitting on the toilet before a new man came on duty. He'd left exhausted and driven home to Encino, some twenty miles away. His wife had greeted him at the front door. "The Boss has just called and he wants you to call him immediately."

Crawford wearily called the Old Man's private number. "Roy? Where the hell have you been? I want you back here right away." From his churlish tone Roy knew something serious had happened.

He raced back over the mountain roads. Hughes was sitting in bed watching a movie when he arrived. He was all solicitous concern by now.

"Roy, I'm glad you could come. I'm terribly sorry I had to call you. But there's something you have to do for me."

He motioned toward the pillow behind him, which rested against the headboard. "Take the tape over there and measure how much this pillow has slipped in the last half hour. You'll see a mark I made with a pencil at eight fifteen."

Roy quietly measured and reported there'd been a four-inch slippage. Hughes made a careful note on the pad on the bedstand. "Thanks so much, Roy. Now go home and get some rest."

By then Hughes had developed a new concern. He was fearful of disposing of his urine or—if not fearful—at least didn't want this elimination of Howard Hughes to go ignominiously down a sewer pipe. He issued orders that it all be saved, and started urinating in jars. As he filled each jar it was solemnly corked and sealed and carried to the château's garage, where it was stored on shelves. When he eventually left years later there were hundreds of jars gathering dust. Obviously the household servants who had this task didn't save all the jars but were cautious to store enough that if Hughes ever checked the garage he'd be assured his orders had been carried out. Periodically he'd send a man to "go count the jars." This became a joke with off-duty people.

Another curiosity attracted the attention of the guards and was the subject of endless speculation. Each week a station wagon would arrive with two huge cartons of Kleenex. The auto would pull up to the service entrance and ten minutes later return to the gate, still with the two cartons in the back. The guards dreamed up fanciful versions of what this operation was all about.

One theory even held that the Old Man was hiding in the boxes and this was his method of moving about.

Eventually they found out the truth. The two new cartons were taken to the Hughes room while old Kleenex and Kleenex boxes were collected, put in the old cartons, carefully sealed with thick tape again and taken out in the station wagon. Why Hughes demanded this secret rite to give the impression the same cartons were moving back and forth no one could discover.

As for the Kleenex itself he used endless sheets of it all day to pick up anything, to rub his body, to spread about, to put objects on. The boxes themselves he utilized as slippers, changing to a new "pair" a half dozen times a day. Finally, he kept a stack of boxes nearby to stack and restack again and again like a child with toy blocks. The cartons with the used boxes and Kleenex were taken directly by the station wagon to Romaine Street, where they were immediately burned in the incinerator as the Old Man had directed.

Another daily ritual was equally odd. A car would emerge and speed off with a small jar to nearby UCLA Medical School each morning and a messenger arrive back a few hours later. Hughes insisted that his feces be analyzed in a lab and a report returned daily. If he couldn't save that, he could at least know of any change in it, he apparently concluded.

His final demand in his dark, sealed command post was a daily report on radioactivity in the Los Angeles air, delivered from an agency each afternoon.

Occasionally Hughes would emerge from his isolated stupor in a wild flurry of angry demands. Chouinard overheard one such shouting tirade when he was in a maid's room next to Hughes' self-made prison one day.

The Boss was talking with one of his attorneys in Los Angeles. Hughes had been lending money to Northeast Airlines, which hadn't been able to meet the payroll. Now he was ready to take it over, he told the lawyer. But his whole scheme hinged upon getting a route from Boston to Miami to make the project profitable.

He wanted the attorney to go to Senator Ted Kennedy and somehow arrange to get the new route. "I don't give a goddamn how much you have to pay him," he shouted at the lawyer, who obviously demurred at such a crass gesture. "I know the Kennedys don't come cheap. All I want you to do is grease his palm enough so we get that route, no matter what it costs." Nothing ever came of the matter.

He would as quickly reverse from such outgoing behavior to a psychotic state that could last for days. One day he called Johnny Holmes, one of his aides, who was off for the day, with a minor instruction concerning light bulbs. He kept repeating the same one-sentence direction over and over again, pausing every ten minutes or so and wandering off to watch television or drink some Poland water but returning to ask, "Are you there, Johnny? Are you there?" Johnny would answer, "Yes." Hughes would begin repeating the sentence again. It went on for nearly eight hours before Hughes hung up.

Hughes invented other games to annoy and distract. One of them involved the simple matter of eating his steak. He had sent down an edict to the cook that not only should the steak come directly off the grill and be served with his salad, tomato juice, and Poland water, but no one must take any steak away that had been cooked before he was ready. It must be thrown in the garbage can. This was at a period when he was declining and had begun to develop the fetish that any part of him or anything that was his must not disappear or be used by anyone else.

He'd plague the cook with this rule. The cook would send word that the steak was ready. He'd say he was watching a television program or quickly pick up the phone and pretend to make a call. Often the cook would dispose of six or seven steaks before Hughes was willing to eat. Then, to be sure no one was hoodwinking him, he'd send someone to the kitchen to check the garbage to be sure all the wasted steaks were in the can. He always kept a careful count.

He kept Romaine Street in a constant panic during these days at the château. They never knew whether to take the initiative or not. It was a classic case of being damned if you did and damned if you didn't. Before he developed his apathy to a marked degree he'd call to make an inquiry and be told the matter at hand had been taken care of and settled. He'd raise hell, demanding to know why he hadn't been consulted, who the hell did they think was running things, and did they want to start looking for new jobs. If someone pressed him for a decision on a similar matter and reminded him that a memo had been sent three months before, he'd go into the same kind of rage. "When I want you to tell me how to run things, God damn you, I'll ask," he'd shout.

Chouinard doesn't know who came up with the idea of starting a new company that could operate on its own, independent of the Old Man. But it was a bold and wild gesture.

Chouinard first heard of it when Romaine ordered guards for an office in Kirkeby Center, a new high rise in Westwood. It didn't even occur to him to ask what it was all about, as he assumed it was another of The Boss's secret ventures.

The office itself had been in the midst of a refurbishing for months and bore the name "Hughes Dynamics." As it was explained to Chouinard, it was to be a separate company that dealt with software computer projects for engineers and architects. Hughes had leased half the top floor and the other half was a restaurant. It was lavishly done, with paneled cabinets and walls, a sunken fountain, and even a fancy office for Hughes that aides studied with amusement. The rugs were so thick they had to be delivered by helicopter. The lease was $3,500 a month.

Soon after, a security routine was started. A Greek Mormon youth who'd come to Los Angeles to attend college was placed on the job as a guard on the night shift.

A few nights later two reporters who'd been drinking at the bar in the restaurant across the hall came out and saw the sign on the door and started making inquiries of the Greek youth. He must have learned that in Greece police took precedence over reporters because he started a terrible fight and physically threw them both out.

The next day newscaster Stan Atkinson called Chouinard. "I just thought you'd like to know that tonight on the eleven o'clock news they're going to talk about that new Hughes operation at the Kirkeby Building, where your guard beat up two reporters."

Chouinard was annoyed but didn't think it anything too serious. He took his time, went for a haircut, and late that afternoon called Romaine to report what was going to happen on the news.

"Holy mackerel!" shouted one Mormon. "Why didn't you tell us sooner? There isn't much time to kill the story."

"Why worry?" he asked. "It doesn't seem that important."

"Great Scott! Don't you understand? The Boss doesn't know we started that company." It had been secretly going on for months; executives had been hired; a manager named Montgomery from TWA had been appointed and Hughes had never been informed.

"Maybe we can somehow pull the plug on the Old Man's television set or screw up the antenna," one Romaine executive suggested.

The worst happened. News of the fracas went on the air. Jean Peters saw the eleven o'clock show and went to the Old Man's room. "I didn't know you had a new company," she remarked.

"God, I don't," he replied. She told him the name, where it was.

He was on the phone to Romaine Street immediately, wanting to know from the panicked Gay what was going on, why hadn't he been told, who did they think they were to start a new business and not tell him?

"I want everyone given two weeks' notice and that place subleased tomorrow," he yelled. "When I want goddamned advice on investments I'll let you know."

The company was destined to have more bad luck. One young genius, when told that he was being fired, was clever enough to go "insane." He stood on a window ledge and threatened to jump. They finally got him off by promising to keep him on the payroll. One more possible scandal about Hughes Dynamics, they thought, would be more than anyone could handle.

John Meier, the opportunist, was still on the payroll years later in Las Vegas. He was in charge of buying mining claims.

CHAPTER 33

IF SUCH EXCITEMENT ADDED SPICE TO THE BEL AIR ERA OF the Hughes saga, the overriding concern in the beginning years was the battle for control of TWA. The enemy faction was trying to flush Hughes from cover and entangle him in the legal battle. As long as he could escape and delay, he held the hole card in the billion-dollar poker game.

There are various drop points where one can keep up with the low gossip of Hollywood. Weekly, Chouinard moved through the Polo Lounge of the Beverly Hills Hotel, the several bars at the Beverly Wilshire Hotel, Scandia, a few of the posh Italian spaghetti joints of Beverly Hills where a plate of linguine can come to eight dollars, Musso-Frank in Hollywood, and the two Schwab's drugstores, on Sunset Boulevard and in Beverly Hills. No one knew nor cared who he worked for or what he did. He was simply Mike Conrad, one of scores of Hollywood hustlers.

Schwab's on Sunset was one of his favorites for breakfast, because he liked not only the corned-beef hash but the conversation with the habitués, which was entertaining. Most were would-be actors, writers, or—if they were really in fantasy land—movie producers with projects to peddle to other impoverished entrepreneurs. Each morning they'd slouch in, pick up the morning *Variety* or *Hollywood Reporter,* order coffee, and start building their daily dream world.

It was at the crowded counter about 9:30 one Sunday morning that Chouinard was to see the character who was to inspire him to start plotting a series of schemes that went on for months. The subject came in wearing unpressed faded blue denims, a blue polyester shell jacket, and a look of melancholic despair that—even if he hadn't looked so much like the Old Man—would have made anyone who'd seen Howard Hughes in the past ten years start with shock. He was nearly the same height, weighed a bit more, and was probably about the same age—say fifteen years ago—Hughes had been when the last photos were taken. Chouinard studied him as he sat at the end of the counter, ordered a Danish and coffee, and started reading the *Times* comics. The hairline? A bit too low and full. The face? Contours much the same but a bit heavier. He put him away under the HH file in the back of his head.

The Hughes forces were all increasingly nervous by then about the widespread tales of Hughes being a psychotic, an invalid, a recluse who couldn't stir. In the past he'd refused to appear in court, worn his eccentric tennis shoes, skipped from one hideaway to the next, met people in old black Chevrolets on lonely roads at three A.M. But by 1963 things were sticky; the vicious TWA fight for control was in full furor. His staff subtly propagandized when they could about Hughes' natural shyness, his disdain for conventional business and legal procedures, his embarrassment concerning poor hearing. But the rumor machine was slowly grinding on with the truth: Howard Hughes had flipped out with his fear of germs.

There were immediate concerns. Chouinard envisioned the

day some enterprising con man, convinced Hughes was a basket case, would start suing Hughes over anything and win by default in the courts. He'd also heard there was a standing $25,000 reward for delivering a subpoena to Hughes on the TWA suit. As some $100,000,000 was immediately at stake, the price was cheap enough. Chouinard wondered what would happen if some process server started a brush fire near the château in Bel Air, forcing the invalid Hughes to vacate, then served him the subpoena. Finally, *Life* magazine was at work on a major Hughes story. It planned to pinpoint the Bel Air château as the place where Hughes was hiding out. Helicopters had been circling with *Life* photographers shooting aerials. More *Life* reporters were hanging around the gates, questioning the college boy-relative guards several times a week. (Chouinard doesn't know whether he was pleased or just amused when the story finally did come out stating Hughes was surrounded by bodyguards worthy of the CIA and FBI combined. He looked at his raffish collection of employees with new awe.)

His guards were just as uninformed about the château as the press. It was useless to question them. They saw food going in, a few visitors coming and going, the doctor passing through the gates each day. But they weren't really sure anyone named Howard Hughes was in there. For years Hughes had been reported here and then there and had always used just such ploys as he moved from home to home. It could simply be the same old game again.

Even as all knew Hughes *must* be in there—the Romaine Street executives, the lawyers, the outside guards—none *really* knew. No one saw him. Documents and papers, memos and project outlines all went in. None came out. His very occasional contact was always by phone, which could be from anywhere.

Chouinard's idea began to take shape. If there was some way to throw TWA sleuths and the press off the spoor, some way to make them think Hughes was simply back to his old tricks, some way to make them suspicious of their own Germ Theory, they could get relief.

Chouinard went to Romaine Street to call on Bill Gay. He'd just worked out rough details of using the Hughes look-alike, but he needed approval. He knew it was useless to try to reach Hughes directly by a memo. If there was any reply, which was improbable, it would be a scribbled "No!"

Gay toyed nervously with a pencil at his desk in his paneled office as Chouinard outlined how he wanted to hire this man and arrange for him to appear here and there as Hughes to confuse everyone. "I can't authorize anything like that," Gay interrupted. It was nutty, dangerous, and The Boss would never go for it. Further, he pointed out, there was probably something illegal, he thought, about going out of your way to avoid a subpoena. It could be interpreted as tampering with the courts, and Hughes could lose the whole ball game. If the double was caught, it could mean the TWA fight would turn into chaos.

"Go talk to Bob Maheu," he said, dismissing Chouinard. "He'll tell you why it won't work." Maheu was riding high in the Hughes hierarchy at the time, and the detective knew Gay was simply covering himself by having Maheu share the responsibility for rejecting the idea.

He called Maheu and drove out to his Brentwood home. Maheu poured a Scotch as Chouinard ran through the idea again. When he'd finished, Maheu hit the coffee table with his fist. "My God, this is a coincidence!" he exclaimed. "I've just been thinking of the same thing myself!"

"Yeah?" the detective replied cynically. "Well, I've already got the double!"

But Maheu was in the wild blue yonder. "We'll charter a seven-oh-seven from Pan Am!" he expanded. "You put a crew of bodyguards around this guy and we'll hit Hawaii first, then Mexico City, and then maybe someplace like Bermuda."

Chouinard could envision Gay's reactions to dropping hundreds of thousands of dollars so casually.

"Let me go back to Bill Gay and tell him you approve."

"Sure—and I'll call him before you get there!" Maheu said.

It was typical that Bill Gay had changed his stance by the time Chouinard arrived. He was fearful and suspicious of Bob's supposed popularity and rumored influence with the Old Man. He grudgingly agreed but still wouldn't give official approval, he said. In effect, it was Chouinard's ass if he fouled up and Gay would grab some of the glory if it worked.

Chouinard's first chore was to find the prospective double again. He didn't know his name, where he lived, any of his background. He only had Schwab's to start with, so he set up a surveillance.

"Look for a guy who looks like Hughes, you'll recognize him when you see him," he instructed the stakeout man, ordering him to stay there all day until he found the double. He gave him one of his Mike Conrad and Associates business cards.

"Just tell the guy to call me, that I have some good news for him," he ordered.

The following Friday his man called in. He'd just delivered the card. Chouinard sat anxiously by the phone all weekend: No call from the elusive fake Mr. Hughes.

Monday morning he settled in at Schwab's himself. It was Wednesday before the prey appeared, shambling in with his usual grim expression for coffee. Chouinard took a stool next to him and asked him if he'd gotten his card. "Oh, so you're Mike Conrad." He turned to look at the detective suspiciously. "What do you want?"

Chouinard told him bluntly he wanted to use him as a Hughes double. They'd decided not to offer him too much money or admit that he would be on the Hughes payroll directly, as they feared he'd boost the price or might even use his employment for a shakedown later. "I don't work for

Hughes, but I want you for this job," Chouinard explained. "I'll pay you a hundred fifty dollars a week."

The man, who told Chouinard he was a screenwriter, shook his head. "Not me! I don't want any part of it. I don't even want to talk about it."

Chouinard kept pleading, pointing out there was no danger and it "will be fun." "What would I have to do?" the screenwriter asked at last. The detective explained. Just a few simple appearances in public places—really just pranks.

Chouinard slowly won his confidence enough that the man suggested they go back to his apartment and talk more. He lived a few blocks away. It was evident from his disheveled quarters that he needed money. One thing caught Chouinard's attention, a half dozen gaudy acrylic paintings of nudes. The screenwriter had done them himself, he said proudly. They looked like the dabblings of an amateur to the detective, but they were a point of contact. Chouinard told him that his wife was a painter and suggested they drive over to his home to see her work. The screenwriter agreed.

As they went through the city to Westwood the man kept ruminating over the detective's offer. "Some jealous husband would probably shoot my ass off," he remarked. "Or the fuzz could arrest me for impersonation or something if we got caught." He was becoming half interested. "My name's Brooks Randall," he finally volunteered.

Over a few drinks at Chouinard's house the detective convinced Randall to give it a try just once. "I'll give you a full week's pay. If you don't like it, you can quit."

Later, Chouinard was to find out the real reason Randall was fearful, much as he wanted money. Evidently, he had a few unpaid bills and he did not want anyone to have his address or know where he could be found.

"I don't like the whole idea," he complained. "I'm a great admirer of Mr. Hughes." It seemed a non sequitur. Chouinard let it pass.

They were now ready to move. The detective called Bob Maheu, who was still enthused about his idea of a worldwide junket, which would have cost a small fortune. "Why don't we try something small to start and knock out any kinks like possible photographers," Chouinard suggested. Maheu pondered this and then agreed it made sense.

One important element in the whole project was to be sure that no actual photo of the double was ever taken. If some newspaper was to run such a picture and it somehow was seen by the Old Man, all hell would erupt. The mission was simply to create gossip and rumor. That way they could always back away and deny anything if Hughes pressed them.

Lake Tahoe seemed to Chouinard like an ideal place for the first appearance. One reason was that rumors had popped up that Hughes had been buying up those amphibious planes and there had been public conjecture that he was planning the small airline from San Francisco to Lake Tahoe for tourists who could then land on the lake. What if they built on this gossip? If Hughes were to appear at Lake Tahoe, for example, to negotiate some land purchases, it would be sure to create attention. They'd function like a guerrilla strike force as Chouinard romantically saw it—emerging, starting a flurry of rumor and conjecture, and then disappearing. It was essential, of course, that they never identify the mysterious, lanky visitor as Howard Hughes. That way, Chouinard reasoned, there could be no legal involvement. "If other people say he was Hughes and we deny it, no one can accuse us of avoiding subpoena," he told Maheu.

He called Brooks Randall and told him not to shave for a few days and to be ready to take a trip. He recruited his father-in-law, Jack Schaller, a distinguished-looking man of seventy-one, to act as a big real estate broker. The rest of his task force included four bodyguards he pulled off regular patrol duty. Also, he arranged with a friend, a Mercedes-Benz salesman, for him and his wife to drive up and join them for an expenses-paid vacation at Squaw Valley. It was to be a trick he'd worked out for an added twist.

Randall and his girlfriend were to arrive on a Saturday morning in a T-Bird the detective had loaned him. Chouinard would go up the day before to set things up. He was afraid to send Randall in the plane, as he thought a pilot might possibly recognize him as Hughes and blow the whole scheme. The others were to come up by commercial airline but use aliases and were not to speak to one another during the trip. He had called ahead and made reservations at a motel for everyone.

Friday, Chouinard arrived early and started making arrangements. First, he hired a driver and a black limousine with darkened windows. Noticing an amphibious plane down at the pier, he rented it for Saturday just in case he needed it. Maybe for a fast getaway!

He cruised along the pine-laden shore with the limousine, making inquiries about different hotels and restaurants where they could stage their scene. They finally settled on a rustic, weatherbeaten old hotel on the north shore.

It seemed ideal. It was far enough away from activity that they weren't likely to encounter anything like police or reporters. They could make a fast departure for their motel. There were just enough guests and tourists to create talk without the threat of a mob scene. Chouinard went in to make inquiries.

The hostess of the cavernous dining room was a garrulous little woman with a French accent, in a printed organdy frock. "I want to arrange a luncheon for two tomorrow afternoon for my boss," Chouinard explained. He pointed to a large, isolated table in one corner. "We'd like that table and the three surrounding it. This is a business meeting and everything must be discreet and very private. He's an important man."

She began describing the menu. It gave him a flash of inspiration. "We won't be dining on your food. We'll bring our own." He added hurriedly, "Of course, price is no object."

She seemed downright puzzled.

"My employer is—well, rather eccentric," he explained weakly.

She murmured an understanding reply and said she'd have to check with the hotel manager but she was sure it would be all right.

"He's meeting with a man up here to discuss some important land acquisitions," he confided. "You understand. We don't even want waiters serving food listening in."

Everything was ready by eleven Friday morning, but then Chouinard began to worry as he strolled about the nearly deserted lobby. What if they went through the whole act and no one recognized the mysterious stranger as Howard Hughes? Maybe he should break his own rules and get a rumor started. He mused over it and then decided it was worth the risk. He could always deny it later.

If there was any way to start gossip in a backwater area he knew it was to tell a switchboard operator. A cute girl was running the switchboard behind the desk. He started chatting with her. She was a dark-haired, attractive, Mexican-American of nineteen, who told Chouinard she was from Berkeley. She also was through work at noon. "Have you ever flown over the lake?" he asked.

"I've never even been on a plane."

He told her of the rented amphibious plane and asked her if she'd like a ride. She was thrilled.

"I'll tell you what!" he continued. "Why don't I have the hotel pack a lunch and we'll have the plane take us to some beach for lunch, then pick us up?"

If she thought he had any romantic motives, she didn't show it. She agreed immediately. They arranged to meet at the pier at one o'clock.

The pilot circled the lake for a time, then landed off a deserted beach on the southwest shore. Chouinard told him to return in an hour and they settled down to fried chicken, potato salad, cold beer, and dessert. They'd been chatting a half hour when Chouinard noticed a small group of girls coming down the beach. He thought little of it until one of the approaching figures seemed somehow familiar. Then he sat up with a start. The girl was the Chouinards' neighborhood baby-sitter! How she had found her way to this particular Tahoe beach at this particular time was more than he could fathom. He suspected a dozen motives: Gay was checking up on him; TWA knew what he was trying to pull.

It all turned out to be innocent coincidence. The girl stopped to talk and went on. She was vacationing before departing with her mother as a missionary to Africa, and this trip was a small present.

After the group left, Chouinard went on chatting with the girl, referring to his boss, tomorrow's luncheon, the big deal he was involved in, and how important it would all be for Lake Tahoe. She nodded and listened politely but it was obvious she wasn't with the Chamber of Commerce. Finally, as he saw the plane approaching for their return, he decided to drop the bait.

"Do you know who my boss is?" he asked. She shrugged.

"Howard Hughes!"

She nibbled on a bit of chocolate cake, then asked shyly, "Who's Howard Hughes?"

Well, he thought as they flew back to the pier, all of us live in our own little worlds.

But he needn't have worried. Their little adventure had excited her enough to relate all the details to other employees the next morning. By afternoon he could tell from the curious glances of the desk clerk and bellhops that they were in on the secret. The smiling French hostess when he went in to inspect the dining room was less reticent. "So! Mr. Hughes is the man!" she said. "I know him. He and Ava Gardner visited here once."

He was in a panic! What if she recognized his "Mr. Hughes" as a fraud and an interloper?

"Then you must know how strange he is," he said. "Please don't act as if you recognize him or come over to the table. He doesn't like that. It really upsets him."

She seemed hurt. "He was always so very nice to me," she pouted.

"But this is different—an important business meeting," he pleaded.

"As you wish, sir," she replied stiffly.

He was on the front steps when his entourage arrived. First a car with the four bodyguards, then the limousine with his father-in-law and Randall, both looking stiff and anxious. He'd instructed them to discuss real estate and acreage costs in the back seat so the local driver would overhear. He doubted if they had.

Ouly a half dozen people were having a late lunch as the bodyguards entered first, looked suspiciously around, then went to take seats at the tables surrounding the corner table. He brought in the box with brown bags containing ham and turkey sandwiches, pickles, potato chips, and soda pop and, as the waiters stared bemused, handed them out to the little group. "Mr. Hughes" took a seat facing the door and adjusted his hearing aid while Chouinard's father-in-law sat beside him and started talking. At other tables diners began to whisper excitedly. It was working.

Within ten minutes the hostess, who knew her own mind, walked over and emptied an ashtray on one of the guards' tables, smiling fetchingly across at Hughes. He glanced up at her with an expression of annoyance, then nodded briskly. She retreated. Chouinard got up and went to her station near the door, trying to hide his anger. He had to find out her reaction. There was no chance to ask.

"My, Mr. Hughes looks grand! Just like he did when he was here with Miss Gardner," she babbled. "But he *has* put on a little weight. He is *such* a lovely person!" Chouinard went back to the table relieved.

Within twenty minutes they were ready to leave. While onlookers lingered over coffee and watched the group, "Hughes" stood up and they solemnly filed out to the cars.

Their next target was ten miles away, a small restaurant at Squaw Valley. They laughed on the way. It had worked! Their first try. They arrived, sat down at tables on a stone patio.

Chouinard's friend the Mercedes salesman, in plaid shorts and a flamboyant straw hat, was sitting with his wife at a patio table, as arranged, drinking wine and chatting. He wore a camera on a strap around his shoulder. They ignored the Hughes entourage as they sat at the far end, talking quietly and taking in the warm sun. Meanwhile Chouinard instructed one of the guards to ease out and sneak to the guard rail to shoot a few pictures of his gathering. Behind them in the parking lot they'd placed a car so the 1963 license plate would show in the photos. He had plans for the pictures later.

They were ready then for the planned incident to create more gossip. Chouinard's garish friend stood up, took his camera, and began to shoot photos of Hughes. Bodyguards rushed toward him, grabbed him, and began to shove him around. His wife shrieked. Terrace waitresses rushed to get the manager. There were shouts, curses, cries. One of the guards yanked the camera away, pulled out the roll of film, threw it to the floor. The manager ran to phone the police. It was over in less than two minutes.

They hurried to their autos and drove away.

The salesman friend, his wife sobbing beside him, refused to file charges when police arrived. Later Chouinard went back to see the restaurant manager and apologize. The manager was outraged.

"I don't see why he didn't file charges and sue that fellow Hughes!"

Chouinard explained: "I found out who he was and we've settled all that so he's happy. You see, he didn't want to raise a ruckus. That woman he was with wasn't his wife."

"Oh, of course," the manager replied. "Now I understand."

There was to be a delightful little addendum to prove their success even before they arrived back in Los Angeles. Juan Trippe, then the president of Pan Am, was vacationing at Lake Tahoe at the time. He called the Romaine Street headquarters late that afternoon. "I understand Mr. Hughes is up here visiting," he said. "Would you tell him I'd very much like to get together and talk with him." He'd never seen him either.

Bob Maheu was delighted and even Bill Gay grudgingly admitted the plan had succeeded. New rumors and press reports were out that Hughes was indeed active and secretly negotiating big real estate deals. As usual, the Hughes organization denied everything. As for Brooks Randall, he'd performed like Laurence Olivier and obviously relished the part.

They arranged for their next foray a week later. It wasn't to be as elaborate as the Tahoe caper but just something to keep the gossip pot bubbling. Chouinard put Randall in dark glasses, and with two bodyguards they flew to San Francisco, where he'd made a reservation at one of the city's most exclusive restaurants.

As before, he ordered an isolated table and one in front of it. He then invited his brother-in-law, who lived in San Francisco, to join them, explaining the event. The relative refused at first, complaining that they'd all go to jail, but finally reluctantly agreed. He arrived with a large briefcase, as Chouinard had instructed. Chouinard went in, looked over the arrangements, and complained about a few petty things such as a bowl of flowers. "My boss has an allergy," he explained.

The maître d' was solicitous but let it be known in a crisp Italian accent that his restaurant catered to a lot more important people than his boss, whoever he might be.

The bodyguards entered, scrutinized the other diners suspiciously, then took their table. The brother-in-law appeared next, with his case, followed by Mr. Hughes. The officious maître d' took one quick glance at his boss and turned to Chouinard. "He can't come in here," he announced with obvious delight. "We serve absolutely no one who isn't wearing a tie."

Chouinard shrugged. "Okay. But do you know who that is?"

The maître d' turned to look again. "Oh, shit!" he gasped, losing his phony Italian accent. He bowed and led Hughes to his table.

Chouinard ordered a round of vodka and orange juice for everyone and an empty glass for Mr. Hughes. Puzzled, the waiters hovered about. Now his brother-in-law ceremoniously opened the briefcase and pulled out a large Thermos. Carefully, he poured the vodka and orange juice his sister had prepared at home into the Hughes glass.

The maître d', aghast with horror, rushed over. "You can't do this!" he announced as diners at nearby tables tittered. "We have the finest vodka in San Francisco. This is against the law!"

Chouinard smiled shyly up at him. "You may have the best vodka. But does your orange juice come from Spain?" The maître d' quietly retreated, standing near the entrance and grumbling to the waiters.

They dined quickly and left. A day later Herb Caen, the San Francisco columnist, had an item about Howard Hughes' peculiar drinking habits.

Back at their hotel, exuberant over the fun they'd had, they decided to strike again that very night. Randall, by now well into his role and the booze, started giving instructions just as if he were Howard Hughes as they set out for Bimbo's, an old-fashioned nightclub.

They ordered one large table near the stage, watched a few girlie acts. Then a beautiful blonde, one Miss January Jones, appeared and sang. She was dreadful. But after she'd completed her show Chouinard scribbled a note on the back of one of his Mike Conrad cards. "Someone here wants to meet you." Like most show people she couldn't resist the bait. And, of course, the rumor of Hughes being there was out. A few minutes later she arrived with her husband. Chouinard made hurried introductions, then casually motioned toward Randall. "And I don't have to tell you who he is," he concluded. She took a chair next to Hughes, and her husband sat next to the detective.

Randall was in his glory. "You were magnificent," he said. "Has anyone told you how much you look like Jean Harlow?"

She giggled. "My daddy back in Oklahoma used to say that all the time."

Then her husband gave Chouinard a jolt that dried up the forty-eight hours of vodka he'd been drinking. "Do you know Bob Maheu? I hear he's with you now. I used to be with him in the FBI."

"Oh, sure," he said. "I work with him all the time."

The husband began to tell anecdotes of their days in the Bureau that left no doubt he was authentic. All Chouinard was thinking was how to get out of Bimbo's fast.

Not Randall, who was becoming increasingly expansive as a fake billionaire. "I've planned for years to do a biographical movie about Jean," he was explaining, "and I think you're just right for the part."

Randall was just elaborating on his production plans when Chouinard got up and went over to whisper in his ear. A few minutes later Hughes announced that it was time to leave for some mysterious appointment. (As far as Chouinard knows, Miss January Jones is still waiting to hear from Hughes. The next day her agent called Walter Kane, whom he knew through the network of agents. "Your boss was up in San Francisco at Bimbo's last night and wants my client to star in his new Harlow movie," he announced. Walter was very confused but said Howard had a great eye for talent.)

The next morning they were all hung over and called room service for some bloody marys. Chouinard started browsing through the Sunday *Chronicle* and came across a fascinating ad. There was a huge yacht for sale in Sausalito, across the Bay. A few more drinks and he decided to act. He dialed the number. "I'm speaking for my employer, who must remain anonymous," he said. "And if he comes over to see the boat everything must be top secret. Is that understood?"

The agent agreed, but explained that the yacht belonged to the president of a steamship line and he could only deal with principals who had been recommended. "Who is your principal?" he asked.

"Have it ready at noon," Chouinard said. "You'll recognize my boss."

There was a stunned expression of recognition on the agent's face when they arrived. He was an astute and eager salesman. He toured them about the ship topside. Then Randall, making churlish comments about the gabby agent not speaking loud enough, demanded to see the engine room. Here he was in his glory as an actor, glaring disdainfully at a smudge of oil here, checking gauges carefully there. Then he turned again to Chouinard. "Ask him if we can take it out for a run," he ordered loftily. The agent hadn't expected this, but it seemed a sale was likely. "It will take a little time to round up the crew," he apologized.

They spent Sunday afternoon cruising the Bay, sipping from the case of champagne the agent had ordered aboard. It was most relaxing. As they got ready to go ashore "Mr. Hughes" asked for another look at the stern. "I was just wondering if there would be any way to modify that to catapult a small seaplane off," he pondered. The agent allowed as how he was sure it could be done. Chouinard said he'd call Monday.

Their final official attack was on Las Vegas itself, where Hughes had been a familiar figure. The earlier triumphs had given them a sense of bravado that demanded new challenges. They flew over and checked into an obscure motel on a Saturday afternoon.

Chouinard went over to the Sands and ordered a good table for the late show, giving the maître d' a hundred-dollar bill.

"My boss wants to come in after the lights are dimmed through the fire-escape entrance and leave the same way before the lights are up." He knew the gossip had already started with his request.

That night they made their entrance quietly. People at nearby tables and waiters were distracted from the show watching the tall figure cupping his ear to hear the comedy act. Their departure was abrupt. The next day the word was out all over Vegas.

Their guerrilla attack had worked beautifully. They'd left a trail of rumor and gossip without being exposed. Chouinard plotted a final grand gesture. They'd suddenly appear at the Long Beach pier, where the controversial Spruce Goose was barned. He'd decided that they'd simply walk up to the guard gate and he'd explain that The Boss wanted to see his plane. He was sure the stunned guards from Hughes Aircraft Division would let them in. He thought it over, however, and decided to drop the whole idea.

They still had those photos the detective had had his guard shoot on the patio at Squaw Valley. They'd studied them and felt they would pass for Hughes well enough if someone only had a brief look.

It was decided that Betty O'Dell, an attractive brunette

who had worked for Chouinard on a few cases, would be the perfect cover. First she called the Los Angeles bureau of *Life* and said she had some recent photos of Howard Hughes, which an auto license in the background would verify. Her husband had been a guard for Mr. Hughes, she explained, and he'd taken them secretly. He'd been fired unfairly soon after, she went on, and they were broke. She wanted to sell them for $1,500.

She was invited to bring them to the *Life* office. She allowed several staffers to study them briefly, then grabbed them back, explaining that she couldn't leave them but that she'd return the next day.

Next came *Newsweek*'s Los Angeles office, where I was bureau chief at the time.

"Is this Richard Mathison?" the female voice asked when I answered the phone. She told me much the same story she'd used at *Life*. I replied that I'd call New York to see if there was any interest and asked when and where I could see them. She suggested Kelbo's, a small restaurant near CBS, at nine that evening. I talked with Gordon Manning, then *Newsweek*'s managing editor, who expressed curiosity but wasn't too interested. He thought the price she'd quoted was high and that it all sounded rather phony, which was my feeling too. It was apparent that *Newsweek* wasn't going to be had.

I called James Phelan, an investigative reporter I knew, who was then working on a Hughes story for the *Saturday Evening Post* and was some years later to be a victim of the Clifford Irving case when Irving stole Phelan's book manuscript and used it as one of his sources for the Hughes "autobiography."

Phelan and I agreed to work out a few details of our own.

We were waiting at a dark table when Betty O'Dell arrived. It was apparent why she'd selected the restaurant. It was done in Hawaiian motif with fishnets and dim lights. We had to strike matches to get a close look at the three photos.

It was the same brief encounter she'd set up at *Life* that afternoon. She grabbed the pictures back and said she'd be in touch the next day if we were willing to pay.

She beat a fast retreat. What she didn't know was that we had a stakeout man of our own, Lynn White, a former Los Angeles deputy chief of police who'd started his own agency after retiring, waiting outside.

She went down the street a half block and a sedan pulled up. She jumped in and drove off. The chase led to a car-rental agency in Burbank where the car was checked in and Betty O'Dell and her driver disappeared in another car.

Phelan followed through. When it was all over it was clear that the Hughes forces were involved. It had been the only break in the cover of the great Doubles Caper.

The flamboyant use of Randall as a double had served its purpose from what feedback Hughes' people could get. At TWA the forces had puzzled over the appearance of the double in public and concluded Hughes indeed was on the move again. While they still considered the château as the prime target to try to deliver a subpoena, they began to search out other likely haunts with their process servers. The press, too, was no longer so sure that the Old Man was hidden inside the Bel Air stronghold.

Until the suit was settled and Hughes got his enormous check, they continued to worry. But the scheme had worked and Chouinard had thrown them off the scent.

As to whether Hughes ever knew of it, one can only surmise that he was never told. There would have been an explosion of some kind. The only person who would have told him was Jean Peters, who by that time was so involved in her own personal difficulties with Hughes that it is doubtful she would have, even if she did hear of it.

CHAPTER

34

HUGHES' MORMONS VIEWED WITH DISDAIN OR DOWNRIGHT horror boozers and smokers. True, a few "jack Mormons" in the organization sneaked coffee, cigarettes, or martinis, but if they were discovered, their advancement was kaput. In this polarized atmosphere there was little difference between a Skid Row alcoholic and the extrovert who went on a spree at a party and ended up with a Sunday morning hangover.

Jean Peters was a constant cause of concern long before she married Hughes. Romaine had heard of her getting bashed at parties and lived in dread of her being arrested and bringing shame down upon the entire Hughes empire. Chouinard was to find himself at odds with this watchful attitude when he and Betty Lou were invited to Jean's sister's wedding not long after he first went to work for Hughes.

That he'd even been invited to the wedding and reception at the Beverly Hills Hotel was a cause for consternation. Within the jealousy-ridden hierarchy news of his mixing at such social levels started a flurry of backstairs gossip at Romaine.

He found Jean pleasant but tense at the reception. He could hardly blame her. For at each corner of the room a Mormon driver stood in a dark suit holding a glass of milk. (One of them was Lavar Myler, whom the detective particularly despised and who years later was to end up on the board of Summa after serving Hughes in his isolated room for nine years.)

Jean explained the situation as she and Chouinard danced. If she was thirsty, she was to walk over to one of the Romaine drivers stationed at each corner of the room and take a sip of milk. The idea of humiliating her in such a way in public outraged Chouinard.

He led her to a fountain where champagne bubbled out and they had a glass, then another.

Myler's face went stony and he signaled angrily to the detective, who refused to respond. Myler put the glass of milk on a nearby table and disappeared. He returned and stalked over to Chouinard. "I just called Bill Gay and told him what you've been doing. He says you aren't to let her have another drink."

Chouinard looked shocked. "No one told me!" he gasped. "And tonight I'm not working."

He was told later his "shocking conduct" had been reported to Hughes in a memo. Apparently the Old Man forgot because it was never mentioned.

In the years between 1962 and 1968 Jean Peters lived a strange existence at Bel Air. She immersed herself in a variety of hobbies. She'd involve herself for a time in furniture refinishing, then send away for catalogs on golf clubs, then lose herself in new parlor games.

At one point she enrolled in UCLA under an assumed name. Hughes was apprehensive as he conjured up images of thousands of college boys. Chouinard received orders to start an immediate surveillance. Spies were to be enrolled in every class she attended and report daily. Chouinard was infuriated. He kept stalling, claiming he couldn't find the right operators for the mission. Finally he was told by Romaine that he could forget it. The operations center had found its own men for the task.

Other times she'd leave Hughes in his isolated room, telling him that she was going to a ballet or an opera with friends. He'd fret and plead but she'd simply ignore him.

The Old Man would have sudden inspirations for lavish gifts. For one of her birthdays he ordered a new Mercedes-

Benz limousine. But it was no ordinary limousine for he'd given instructions for all the upholstery in the mint car to be torn out and replaced with special sanitized, germ-free leather, and then he'd ordered a complete new paint job. For the presentation he had a germ-free driver bring the auto to the front of the house and park it with a rope fencing it off at some five feet distance.

As she cared nothing for luxuries she was hardly polite. After staring at the car for a moment she turned to one of Chouinard's germ-laden guards. "Larry, go put that in the garage, will you," she said. The Old Man's expensive and painstaking precautions were ruined in minutes.

He'd tried similar gestures before. At one point he'd given her a magnificent Packard convertible, now a classic. It was apparently too ostentatious for her and was stored in the Beverly Hills Hotel garage for years. She never drove it.

Sometimes, however, she'd have her own flurries of concern over cleanliness. She'd be particularly outraged at the Hughes cook, who had a way of covering the kitchen with grease as he fried those discarded steaks each day. One Sunday morning a guard, Larry Lewis, called Chouinard at home.

"I've got a problem," he explained. "Mrs. Hughes told me to go buy a new mop, but I don't have the money."

Chouinard instructed him to come to his house and he'd give him the cash. But when he arrived, the detective found he too had only some small change. He approached the maid who was at work at his home and borrowed five dollars. By noon Mrs. Hughes was busily washing down the kitchen.

One of the most confusing facets of the Hughes personality while confined to his sealed, self-imposed exile in Bel Air those many years was his business acumen at certain times. It was as if there was a switch in his head that would click on and off for no apparent reason. After weeks of silence, with memos and paperwork stacking up on the nightstand beside his bed, he would be triggered into a frenzy of activity, calling

Bill Gay, Maheu, and others, with a wide-ranging set of orders, instructions, and detailed analyses. His attention would often concern itself with minutiae on relatively unimportant problems. If there was any priority in his sudden surges of interest, it was too obscure for most to understand.

Typically, he'd call about the guards at the front gate. Or, "I notice the leaves are beginning to drop from the trees. What about the gutters out there? Are there leaves stacked up in them?" Naturally, whoever answered hadn't noticed and would equivocate.

"Well, I want someone out there with a broom every day, cleaning them up," he'd continue. "People are coming in and out of here all the time and I don't want them bringing a lot of dirty, sodden filth into the house." He'd then go on with a rambling dissertation about guards checking their shoes before they came to work to be sure the soles were clean.

He'd get agitated if anything upset one of his rituals such as watching old movies on television. In a high state of indignation he started calling everyone on the staff once when there was a power failure in the Bel Air area at 12:30 A.M. As usual, Bill Gay was held responsible for the power company's problem. Hughes wanted action! During the red alert Romaine found a man who rented gas generators and coaxed him to get out of bed and rush to Bel Air with one of his units. It wasn't a simple installation. Dawn was breaking when the emergency generator began to function correctly while The Boss paced and cursed in his room.

Hughes had a barber, who owned a small shop on Fairfax Avenue, whom he'd kept on standby for some years. When he moved to the Beverly Hills Hotel he suddenly decided he needed the man full time. It seemed odd, as he already was beginning to show signs of fear of anything—hair, nails, or elimination—getting away from him. Then someone realized he was also probably fearful of the barber using scissors or combs used on anyone else on the Hughes hair—even if he didn't intend to have his hair cut constantly.

Negotiations started. The barber was a waspish, older man who'd had his shop for years and didn't want to give it up. Hughes persisted. Eventually a deal was struck. The barber was to come to the hotel each morning and stay until five each day and would be paid five hundred dollars a week.

He arrived regularly each day with his bag and took a seat. He read magazines, did crossword puzzles, listened to the radio. Days passed. He began to pace the floor. "Is Mr. Hughes ready for a haircut yet?" he'd ask.

Each day he'd be given the same answer. "No. Mr. Hughes has said not today, but be sure to be here tomorrow."

Weeks went on. Hughes, meanwhile, became more and more anxious about having his hair cut and started inventing excuses each day to escape Jean's nagging to do something about the untidy hair.

It was nearly a year before relief came for Hughes from the daily harassment over his prospective haircut. It came in the form of the frustrated barber demanding a raise to one thousand dollars a week to continue doing nothing.

Hughes had won. He'd never have his hair cut now! He fired the barber and the next day called Romaine.

"I want you to go up to Utah in the sticks and look around for a barber. Some young fellow who's never heard of Howard Hughes. See if he can come down here. Don't tell him who he'll be working for and offer him seventy-five dollars a week so he won't think he's working for anyone very important." He paused, then explained in a whining voice. "These god-damned barbers around this town seem to think I'm made of nothing but money."

The trip to Utah to find a naive, young barber was never made. Jean Peters solved the immediate crisis that day by storming into the room and cutting Hughes' hair herself while he squirmed and bitched. Soon after they moved to Bel Air, and haircuts became taboo.

CHAPTER 35

IN THE BEL AIR ERA A VARIETY OF ACTIVITIES, ALL CENtered around the best way to escape process servers, created their own odd complications.

During that time Chouinard arranged to pay Jack Hooper, who was in charge of the official Bel Air patrol, four hundred dollars a month to have his men's cooperation. It was a waste of money. The Bel Air patrol was made up of retired cops who were more fearful of the dark and animals than Chouinard's callow striplings.

One aging Irish patrolman who refused to get out of his car after dark explained: "There's this fox that keeps coming up to me and staring in the window and just baring its teeth. He scares me to death."

The neighbors, too, could be a concern. Once Chouinard was called at home. One of the guards had heard strange noises in the brush and thought it might be a process server trying to sneak in. The detective rushed to Bel Air, went up to the area, and started moving stealthily through the bushes. Some noise may have alerted the neighbor because a man suddenly appeared in a flannel bathrobe with a pistol that, at the moment, seemed as huge as a shotgun. Chouinard managed to sneak away but was as wary as his men of going into the brush at night after that.

There were other ways of dealing with some of the process servers besides just avoiding them. Maheu had his sources of information and contacts back East. One unfortunate landed at the Los Angeles airport full of enthusiasm that he was going to pin the tail on the donkey in Bel Air. He got no farther than the off-ramp when he was picked up for carrying counterfeit money. He howled that it had been planted on him and he'd been framed. But who knows? It's such a commonplace cop-out with criminals.

If everyone had collected lore and tales of The Boss's antics and habits, only the old drivers in his quarters had seen him. They were strangely and uniformly mute about his appearance, as if people were asking about some delicate personal matter that was none of their affair.

About 3:30 one morning Bob Roberts was on patrol on the grounds when he noticed the drapes on the big sliding glass doors of the Hughes room weren't completely pulled. There was a small crack near the bottom, where they were supposed to meet.

With a surge of daring he determined to try to get a look at The Boss. He crawled through the rosebushes, took off his shoes, crept to the window, and got down on his knees.

As he described it later, he began to shiver.

The Old Man sat in a straight-backed chair staring vacantly at a wall. He had a napkin spread over his groin but was otherwise naked. Bob judged he weighed perhaps a hundred pounds, an emaciated skeleton such as in films of the survivors of Dachau. Long hair, white and dirty, hung to the middle of his back and a straggly white beard had grown down to the middle of his chest. But the most frightening shock to Roberts were the long curved fingernails and toenails, which he described as five or six inches in length. He stared in horror for a few minutes while the Old Man sat in a yogalike trance, then he tiptoed away.

The next day he told others of what he had done. What

he'd seen was, in a way, what they'd expected. Yet to confront the specter as Bob had was more than he wished. "I could just kick myself in the ass for doing it," he said. "It would have been a lot better never to know." Everyone understood after that why the old drivers preferred not to say anything.

The doctor arrived up to seven times a day to visit Hughes, who was his only patient. He lived in nearby Coldwater Canyon, only a few minutes away. In addition to these constant visits Hughes would call him repeatedly, describing new symptoms. It was a delicate patient-doctor relationship, and as the years passed Chouinard understood why the doctor became an alcoholic. The doctor's first problem, for example, was that he had strict orders never to speak to Hughes when he was visiting him. The Old Man would talk but the doctor had to reply by scribbling notes on a pad and handing them to Hughes. Naturally, too, the Old Man wouldn't allow the doctor to touch him, which made examination rather difficult. He was suffering by then from dreadful hemorrhoids and would sometimes stretch out on the floor and try to stuff them back into his anal canal with those long-nailed fingers while the doctor stood by writing instructions.

Hughes was convinced after a time that he also had a serious heart ailment of some sort. He insisted on always having several large tanks of oxygen in the room with its sealed window. As he was also fearful of bathing and washing his perspiration down the drain, there was a fetid, vile odor in the airless room. His solution to this was to now and again turn the valve and let some tanked oxygen freshen the room.

Chouinard was standing by in the maid's room next to Hughes' one evening when he heard the only eruption Hughes ever to his knowledge had with Jean Peters. She'd come into the room and exploded over the foul odor.

"You're going to have to open a window and let in some fresh air no matter what!" she cried.

Hughes went into a rage. "No, no, no!" he shouted. "Don't

dare to try to open one of those windows!" There was total fear in his voice.

She went out and slammed the door in despair.

As time passed he paid less and less attention to the outside world. The ever-present memos from Romaine stacked higher and higher on his nightstand, and he only made a desultory effort to look at them every few weeks. He refused more and more phone calls and seldom made a call himself. To Chouinard's knowledge the last call he took was from the president of the Bank of America, who was pleading for payment of a million-dollar loan Hughes owed.

His earlier disdain for being told anything became a total fixation, and he'd go into a rage if anyone tried even to suggest he look at some urgent memo or come to some decision. Only when he'd call to make an inquiry about something were his executives allowed to reply.

At Romaine things were in chaos. Demands for answers to questions involving millions of dollars came in constantly. All the Hughes executives could do was procrastinate, just as the Old Man was doing. No one wanted the thankless chore of confronting The Boss with the urgency of any situation.

Then Maheu did a startling thing, which left the Mormons more distraught. Bob called Hughes to say he had to go to Mexico on some urgent business.

The Old Man said he couldn't, that he needed him around.

Maheu hung up, went to Mexico, completed his mission, and called Hughes when he returned to tell him what he'd done.

Rather than reacting furiously, The Boss simply said, "Fine, fine, I'm glad you took care of all that." He somehow respected Bob for disobeying his orders. From then on the Maheu star became increasingly brighter.

Others wondered what caused The Boss's rapid decline at that time. They'd all seen the slow changes, his growing phobia concerning germs, the increased procrastinations, but it seemed that his moments of lucidity were becoming fewer with each passing week. Chouinard was to get one partial medical answer by a circuitous means.

Hughes' doctor's father-in-law died in Kansas City. Hughes was deeply upset when the doctor approached him to request that he accompany his wife to the funeral in the Midwest.

"No, no," he replied. "You can't do that. I'll send my best man to take her and see she's all right."

The doctor and wife reluctantly agreed. Chouinard was ordered to go with her and bring her back.

Now Hughes called Romaine with orders for Chouinard. He showed some of his old enthusiasm for intrigue. "I think that doctor's telling his wife about my condition. I want Jeff to find out just how much she knows and what he's said. Tell him to see if he can find out."

Chouinard and the doctor's wife hit it off splendidly on the flight to Kansas City. He found out her first husband had been a fighter pilot on the *Yorktown* and had been killed flying an F4F. Chouinard knew all about the unit. Over martinis the talk turned to Hughes quite naturally, and it was soon obvious she knew a great deal about the case from her husband. It was her husband's opinion, she explained, that Hughes had suffered a serious nervous breakdown when he finally lost control of TWA, his prized toy in his collection of companies. If he'd been treated properly, the doctor maintained, he could have recovered. But he never had been. No one would force the issue with him, and the result was that Hughes had been left a psychogenic cripple. It was as good a theory as anyone was ever to get.

As for Chouinard, his mission was aborted. He delivered the wife to Kansas City and put her in a limousine. He then took off with a bottle of Scotch to visit an old service buddy and never caught up with her again.

When she returned, the doctor told Hughes of Chouinard's disappearance. Hughes wouldn't talk with Chouinard when he tried to give his report. He had mistreated that poor woman in a time of grief, the Old Man complained.

The day came when a brokerage firm delivered the check for the sale of the TWA stock for $540 million. Someone said it was the largest check ever written and the largest ever received by one person.

The executives at Romaine Street were in raptures plotting investments. Some went to look at ranches while others advocated savings and loan firms. Still others saw new industries in Hughes' bright crown of companies. They did, just then, owe the Bank of America $1 million, but that seemed minor.

The Old Man settled it quickly. "I want that money put in the safe in Houston," he ordered. "No investments. Don't even pay the Bank of America with it."

It was an unhappy moment. But even then, it seemed, Hughes had secretly decided to buy up Las Vegas.

During those years no one saw the Old Man except Jean Peters, the old drivers who worked as aides, and one outstanding exception. He was a nine-year-old boy, the son of one of Jean's former secretaries, Sally Macon. She had come to visit and brought the lad. While Sally and Jean chatted, the boy started wandering about the house, eventually coming to the ominous door with the red light above. It obviously was too much of a temptation and he turned the knob.

Hughes was stretched out, surrounded by his Kleenex boxes and oxygen tanks in the dimly lit bedroom. He had a towel over his middle and was watching television.

The youth stood transfixed staring at the beard and hair, the long toenails. It was a moment of mutual horror for both of them.

"Holmes!" Hughes cried to the aide on duty. Holmes came rushing out of his station in the bathroom.

"What is it?" the Old Man demanded.

"A little boy," answered Holmes in bewilderment.

"Well, get it out of here but don't hurt it!"

The boy was ushered back to Sally and word was sent out that security was getting lax and things had to be tightened up. It had to be the first time the Old Man had seen a child in many years.

The day came that Hughes announced to Jean that he was going to a clinic. She'd been after him for years and—as it later turned out—his decision, it seemed, was dictated by the fact that unless he did something the marriage would fall apart.

He made a variety of other promises to soothe her, none of which he kept or probably intended to keep. He told her that they'd leave California for tax reasons and buy a farm in upstate New York, which was one of her dreams. During the trip to the clinic in Boston he told her he'd arrange to start looking for the farm—as Chester Davis, Hughes' attorney, already had a horse farm there—and, if he could find a suitable one, he'd send for her to look it over.

That wasn't all. He explained that they could have a yacht and cruise up and down the coast and spend the winters in Florida if she liked. It was all very glowing and lovely. Everyone noticed a complete change in Jean's mood.

In retrospect it was a cruel and brutal farce, as Hughes even then was obviously secretly plotting his invasion of Nevada. One of his favorite lines in negotiating, after driving the enemy to helpless rage with his stalling and nit-picking, was "I won't negotiate with a gun at my head." Clearly, he was now cornered by marital problems and had fallen back on his tried and true techniques of stalling.

Hughes departed for Boston in a special Pullman car, the entire operation wrapped in secrecy. He reportedly arrived at the clinic, although some claimed he went directly to Las Vegas. Weeks passed and Jean waited. At last she took a plane to Boston to see what was going on at the clinic.

She waited for four days to see him while spokesmen tried to explain that he couldn't see her. Furious, she left and returned to Bel Air. Her rage and frustration exploded at times. One night a guard called Chouinard. "There's shooting going on up at the house," he shouted. "You'd better get here fast!"

The detective was panicked. It could be anything, but nothing good. The phone rang as he was dressing. Romaine had already checked it out. Jean had answered the phone and explained blithely, "Oh that . . . I was just doing some target practice in the attic." The next morning there were bullet holes in the copper roof.

About that time Stan Hough, now a widower, began to visit her at the château. The visits became more frequent, and soon she was going out to dinner. Chouinard methodically reported each visit to Romaine, assuming the report went on to wherever Hughes might be. Then word came that Hughes had bought the lavish Krupp ranch outside Las Vegas for Jean, and a mansion in the town itself.

At Bel Air the Hough visits continued. In Las Vegas it seemed clear that the Old Man had isolated himself in a tiny room on the top floor of the Desert Inn and that Maheu was in charge of the growing enterprise of buying up Las Vegas with the assistance of memos from Hughes, the boss he'd never seen.

At the Bel Air château, gossip had it, Jean Peters had told her husband that she'd never put a foot in the state of Nevada.

CHAPTER 36

JEAN'S DATES WITH HOUGH CONTINUED, AND CHOUINARD'S crew continued to report them to the detective, who passed the information on to Romaine. Then a volcanic eruption came. The Hough visits had not been reported to Hughes by Romaine, but somehow the Old Man had found out.

He called Chouinard in a blazing rage. "We've called Romaine and reported every visit," Chouinard replied.

Hughes hung up but now Romaine was calling Chouinard, accusing the detective of his failure to make clear the romantic implications of it all. In an effort to pass on the blame for not having told Hughes, Romaine said weakly that Chouinard "made it sound like old-friend stuff." The turmoil went on for a few days before the Old Man fixed the blame on poor Bill Gay once again.

Jean moved out of Bel Air soon after to a small house on Maple Drive in Beverly Hills and began divorce proceedings. She later married Hough.

The news of Hughes' entrenchment in Las Vegas had filtered back slowly to Romaine. In the *Rashomon*-like atmosphere, everyone had his own version of how it had all come about, what it meant, what the future held.

No one was quite sure when Hughes had first decided on the massive attack upon the economy of Nevada. There was talk of tax benefits, of Bob Maheu being a Svengali who'd lured The Boss into the enterprise. No one knew.

Chouinard received word that Hughes wanted him to move to Las Vegas. The prospect was far from appealing. Chouinard knew Maheu would be in complete charge and eclipse everyone else. The thought of just standing guard duty wasn't attractive. The old days of trying to keep tab on all those girls may have been ludicrous but they weren't boring. Moving to Las Vegas was distasteful. Chouinard wrote a note to Hughes saying he wanted to quit. It was sent through Romaine, but Chouinard doubts that Hughes ever saw it. There was only silence.

He continued contact with old associates in the Hughes empire. He chuckled sympathetically when he heard of Jack Hooper's dilemma. The one-time head of patrolmen for Bel Air who'd been on Chouinard's payroll had gone on to a full-time job in Las Vegas. One of his first assignments was to guard the Krupp ranch, which the Old Man had bought. There had been the usual orders. No one, absolutely no one, must get near the property. Hooper had made the error of secretly showing a friend around the place one day and had the misfortune of falling into the empty swimming pool and breaking his leg. Chouinard could imagine Hughes' questions when the Old Man got the news. What time of day had it happened? Was Hooper alone? What hospital had he been taken to for treatment? Who had driven the ambulance? Was he alone when help arrived?

Other rumors drifted out. Word came that the racing plane was going to be given to the Smithsonian and the flying boat was to be cut up or given to the City of Long Beach as a tourist attraction. Chouinard had his own interpretation of this gossip: The day Hughes gave up his planes he had lost all control.

He called Kay Glenn. Before he could even ask, Glenn groaned and explained: "I know what you're going to ask. I've had twenty thousand calls and I've never even seen the flying boat myself." Yet they both knew that Hughes had never overcome his bitterness over the ridicule of his plywood plane and the ignominious name the press had given it, "The Spruce Goose." He would never allow it to become a public circus.

Meanwhile one could guess that Hughes was emerging from his apathy. As he acquired more and more Las Vegas property and hotels the time came when there were just no more for sale. He then started buying vacant lots with the explanation that he wanted to keep down the growth of the area.

He seemed to be immersing himself in politics. He had given a huge campaign contribution to Republican Paul Laxalt, who was Governor then, and even talked of backing him for the presidency, Hughes insiders claimed.

The atomic testing near Las Vegas became a cause célèbre with Hughes. The story came out that Hubert Humphrey had been given fifty thousand dollars to aid Hughes in the effort to stop the nuclear test explosion in 1968. The cash had been left in the back seat of Humphrey's auto, Maheu claimed. The Senator denied it all.

Hughes in one memo threatened to "ally myself completely with the all-out anti-bomb factions throughout the entire U.S. . . . this group has only been waiting for a strong leader and I am ready to dedicate the rest of my life and every cent I possess in a complete no-quarter fight to outlaw all nuclear testing of every kind and everywhere."

The claim was that the Old Man was afraid the nuclear tests would keep the tourists away from Las Vegas. But Chouinard recalled how Hughes had demanded a radioactivity report each day when he was secluded in Bel Air. Romaine's jealous gossip held that Hughes was becoming more and more disenchanted with Maheu because he'd failed to stop the tests, an impossible assignment for anyone.

Even when Chouinard had left Hughes' employment, he was still to see a demonstration of the great, hidden power of the Old Man. At one point Chouinard decided he'd try to go into the silver-mining business. He tried to interest some of his old Hughes associates. Chester Davis, the Hughes attorney, called him. He tried to dissuade Chouinard from such an enterprise, explaining that a New York City silver expert, his friend Charlie Engelhard, had told Davis there was a new discovery on the way to develop film, and silver nitrate—one of the biggest uses of silver—wouldn't be needed anymore. Chouinard, an admitted novice in the world of international finance, was impressed. Later he was to find out that everyone at the top of the Hughes empire knew the price of silver was going up; Hughes had been buying up every silver mine available in Nevada, though due to later foulups and confusions Hughes wasn't to make a killing either.

Now and again little blips of information would become official. In 1971 Howard Eckersley, one of Hughes' aides, was a witness in a Nevada lawsuit. He didn't tell much: that Hughes had chosen his self-made prison atop the Desert Inn; that there were five aides in attendance, four of them Mormons; that his way of life was much as it had been in the château in Bel Air.

Word came that Hughes had bought the Las Vegas television station from Hank Greenspun, publisher of the Las Vegas *Sun*. The old-timers thought they knew why. Hughes could now run old movies all night on the station. He planned also, it was claimed, to have closed-circuit television cameras trained on the shows and probably into the dressing rooms, in the hotels he owned, so he could keep track of what was going on backstage.

The memorable day Hughes spoke to reporters over the radio to prove he had nothing to do with the fake Clifford Irving manuscript purported to be his autobiography left Chouinard puzzled. "That has to be Howard Hughes," he told his wife as he listened in amazement. "It's his exact style of talking, just as Hughes sounded years and years ago." When Chouinard had last worked for Hughes the voice was high-pitched and whining. Yet here was Hughes' voice, calm and sober as it had been in the 1950's.

Maheu was to sue Hughes for comments made during that broadcast, but Romaine seems to have prepared for it. A friend told Chouinard, "We took out libel insurance just before Hughes went on the air."

Added mysteries emerged during the Las Vegas days. Hughes was reported in London. It was claimed he was flying about England. Most remarkable of all, there was a news story that the Old Man had gotten a haircut in London and left a large tip!

This era in Hughes' life was to create endless speculation. The questions went on and on. Had the Old Man emerged from his illness completely? Scores of handwritten memos to Maheu would indicate he was busy at his old game of dissecting details. Was he really where gossip claimed he was, flying around the world? Was he really dead? Was there someone else up in that tiny room atop the Las Vegas hotel and was Hughes in South America or Bermuda or Mexico? Was he really well again and were all the tales of his desperate sickness a coverup and sham?

Then came the announcement of his death aboard a plane from Mexico bound for Texas. The fingerprints of the body were those of Howard Hughes. An autopsy was to follow, the results of which are a deep secret.

Howard Robard Hughes left his mark as a daring pilot, a shocking moviemaker, a captain of industry, and a weapons maker who met the challenges of the electronics age.

He had his early moments of glamour. There was the time he was a dashing youth in his blue jacket and gray flannels, sporting a carefully trimmed moustache, his hair neatly parted and slicked down with greasy kid stuff. He danced and laughed, drank rum and Coca-Colas as he wooed the lovelies. Only a few remain who knew that Howard Hughes.

He died leaving an estimated $2.5 billion, although no one is very sure and, unless a will is found, the estate will pay the largest inheritance tax in history, $1 billion or more.

During those final days secret conflicts continued to emerge as jealousies flared over special interests and different entities clashed. The Hughes Medical Institute had taken over Hughes Aircraft Company, which, in turn, owned half of Theta Cable, a television-subscriber system in Los Angeles. Summa, the "umbrella" company formed in 1972, operates today in the Hughes tradition in a heavily secured building near the Strip in Las Vegas, where an array of guards scan closed-circuit television sets tracing every visitor's moves. In Encino another enclave of the empire operates quietly.

Representatives of Hughes' Texas relatives are in control. Bill Gay is finally on top, running operations. Chester Davis, Nadine Henley, Kay Glenn are still on hand. It would seem a steady effort is going on nowadays to put the Hughes house in order.

Summa has a variety of operating divisions. One includes the casinos and hotels in Reno, the Bahamas, Las Vegas; a television station, and a TV network that sends out special reports. The second involves helicopters, Hughes Airwest, and a firm that repairs aircraft. Still another concerns land management, some 1,200 mines in Nevada as well as 30,000 acres of undeveloped desert around Las Vegas. An architectural firm is an added fillip.

Some one hundred scientists get about a million dollars a year from the Medical Foundation to be "medical investigators"—a term Hughes must have devised himself—rather than to do research under regular grants.

Opinion is mixed as to his business acumen. Considering that he started with only $750,000 in 1924 and ended up with billions it would seem he was one of the brightest businessmen of all time. But many inside the Hughes empire disagree. Only when he left them alone did they prosper, some claim. Toolco was a wellspring of money because Hughes had no interest in dabbling in it. For decades it continued to pay fifty cents on the dollar, its profits seeding all other efforts. RKO and TWA, which had his full attention and preoccupation, both ultimately failed for him in their own way. In both cases executives or stockholders revolted against the Old Man's meddling.

Hughes died at seventy. It appears he was not greatly mourned by anyone. At Hughes Aircraft his death was marked with some token gestures of mourning but little talk. At Summa, among the hierarchy, there seems to have been a subdued sigh of relief that the dreadful years of confusion were at last over. People at Hughes Airwest, the Medical Institute, operators of his television station, his hotel in the Bahamas, his architectural designing firm, Hughes Helicopters, Theta Cable television were indifferent except to wonder if his death might affect their own personal fates.

Over martinis his old cronies and associates probably brought up a few more of the endless personal anecdotes of his mad ways. Most probably found it hard after all those years of contact with him to feel any emotion—hate, sympathy, sorrow. He was a man no one knew.

If a middle-class American ran his business and personal life as Hughes did for years, he'd be fired and probably tucked away in a mental hospital. Yet Hughes was dutifully described as "brilliant," "eccentric," and a "genius" for years.

Hughes was no genius. His wealth grew, thanks to employees and the value of the dollar, out of all proportion to his personal contribution. One can only guess—as with all famous and fascinating psychotics—what he might have done had he been well and sane. As it was he was the skunk at the lawn party in his own corporate world. His massive and repeated failures were carefully forgotten, his insane expenditures and self-indulgence swept under the rug. In these days of Sexual Liberation Hughes' extravagant peccadilloes with the ladies seem silly, sexual comic opera almost beyond belief.

Hughes was a lonely, tortured, and unhappy man. Like the mystics of history who went into the desert for forty days for purification, Hughes took his candy bars and went into screening rooms or self-made solitary confinement trying to find inner wisdom and strength. Yet he never matured much past trying to have fun with his playthings, be they planes, companies, or women.

Like most spoiled, lonely little boys who have too much, he didn't have much of that fun. Because he had too much.

ABOUT THE AUTHOR

RICHARD MATHISON was born in Boise, Idaho, and attended the University of Idaho and George Washington University. He was an Operations Officer at Guadalcanal, Munda, and elsewhere in the South Pacific, and retired in the Marine Corps Reserve as a Major. After World War II he joined the Associated Press as a feature writer. Then in 1947 he became Managing Editor of *Fortnight,* a California news magazine. He assigned reporters to a variety of Hughes stories. In 1958 he worked briefly for the *Los Angeles Times* and then became Los Angeles Bureau Chief for *Newsweek,* where the Hughes saga continued. Over the years he has gathered Hughes stories from hundreds of people. He has written three other books and ghosted the memoirs of Oscar Levant, Dr. Thomas Sternberg, Vincent Hallinan, Art Linkletter, and Jack Kelly.